JOHN DANTE'S INFERNO, a Playboy's Life

BY THE SAME AUTHOR

The Mediterranean Runs Through Brooklyn

Valentino and the Great Italians

Conversation with Johnny

Bart: a Life of A. Bartlett Giamatti

Anita Garibaldi, a Biography

The Little Sailor, a Romantic Thriller

Toni Cade Bambara's One Sicilian Night, a Memoir

John Dante's Inferno, a Playboy's Life

Dante in Love

Immigrants, according to Anthony Valerio (vols. 1 & 2)

Semmelweis

"An Infernal Pleasure

This is a highly original way of telling the story of John Dante, self-made namesake of the more famous Dante. Using the medieval poet's vision of Hell as a kind of running parallel narrative, Anthony Valerio weaves a fascinating tale of ambition, excess, friendship, and rocking good times back in the day of the Playboy Clubs, replete with Bunnies, orgies, and hedonistic fun. Valerio writes with verve and compassion about men and women who ran after their dreams and their pleasures with abandon, living as if youth, potency, and beauty would never end. They did, of course, and this gives a poignant quality to the book. This is also the life story of an Italian American who came up from very humble origins to the heights of Hugh Hefner's sexy Never Never Land. I didn't always like these players' choices, and the machismo of that world is sometimes hard to take. Women are prized for their long, smooth legs, their willingness to service the men, their decorative essence, all of which is not the most admirable way of viewing women. But those were the times and those were the values that dominated Hef's universe. John Dante did have his own moral code, unusual as it was, and he was above all a good and faithful friend. Valerio is so expert at making us feel the lives of others, even those very far from our own experiences, and his colloquial style is just right. It seems that he wrote this book out of friendship, and so it is ultimately a kind, compassionate book. I am looking forward to many more tales told by the master storyteller, Anthony Valerio!"—Rebecca West, professor, University of Chicago

"Gripping, Literate, Naughty Bawdy—
Anthony Valerio's biography of John Dante, Hugh Hefner's second-in-command at *Playboy* and the Great Libertine's best friend for over 40 years, is like no other book I have read. Deft and clever, literate and highly readable….Parading through these pages are some of the best-known names in show business and, its darker side--especially for a magazine self-identified as "men's entertainment"-- pornography: Beatty, Bogdanovich, Caan, Cosby, Curtis, Jagger, Lovelace, Nicholson, Reems, Steinem, and, especially, Silverstein. Readers will be riveted by the portrait

of the beloved children's author that emerges in these pages. Not exactly what they may have expected. Silverstein urged John Dante to contact Valerio, whom Silverstein knew and whose work he respected, so that John Dante could write a book--the insider's view of *Playboy!*--that would earn him cnough money to get him to Florence, the town that exiled his namesake, the poet Dante Alighieri close to 700 years earlier. The 20th-century (John) Dante gets to Florence all right, but the price is steep, indeed. It's not exactly "Se7en,"but it has its dark, seamy, *nasty* side. Think *Star 80*. The surprising portrait of Silverstein is but one of the gifts that this book offers. Another is the gangsta Chicagoland of the 1950s and early `60s, which teems with memorable gangland characters. Part biography, part immigrant story, *John Dante's Inferno* in some ways mimics the Poet Dante's imagined journey through hell, into purgatory, and, finally, into paradise. Yet the 20th Century was a chaotic one, and sometimes it's difficult to keep separate what is hell and what is heaven. For example, John Dante claims to have had 16,000 women--and, "maybe", one male--as lovers (he can't be sure: he was too stoned to say, exactly). Heavenly, to be sure, at least as far as John Dante was concerned. Heavenly, but with a (hellish) price to be paid. Valerio writes surely and gives us gripping and very, very literate prose. It seems completely appropriate that the readers of *John Dante's Inferno* be brought into the presence of the Great Libertines of western culture, which include, surely, Casanova and Hugh Hefner. Read it. And enjoy."—Daisy H., university professor.

"He's just crazy enough. He knows his characters. He knows his craft. He gets in and he gets out. It's what good writing should be."—Shel Silverstein

ANTHONY

VALERIO

JOHN DANTE'S INFERNO

A Playboy's Life

To John and Shel, in friendship and gratitude.

Special heart-felt thanks to Noel Cunningham (1949-2011), chef/philanthropist extraordinaire and great colleague & friend of John Dante's.

CONTENTS

①

I realize that the commercial interest in this book lies in the fact that I've known Hugh Hefner for 50 years — and lived with him for 26 of those years.

But I intend the story to be biographical. That is — that a portion of the book be devoted to a checkered, but interesting, journey that led me, inexorably, to meet this complex and fascinating man.

done

At a very early age I had a tremendous affinity for women — and it seems to me now, in retrospect, that at every deciding crossroad in my life a woman

John Dante, courtesy John Dante, personal archive

PROLOGUE

We were at the Dante Café in Greenwich Village, U.S.A., Shel Silverstein and I, mid-1990s. We were friends, colleagues, confidantes. Sotto voce so that even the Italians in the place couldn't hear, Shel began:

"There's a good friend of mine living in a hellhole down in Fort Lauderdale, John Dante, and he wants to write a book about his life in Playboy. I told him about you. I gave him a copy of you *Valentino and the Great Italians*, and he said he liked it and would like to meet you. Just go down and sit around and talk."

This friend John Dante, née Giovanni Aimola, and I were both Italian, loving women, pasta and song. Just by sitting around and talking, all that John Dante had experienced would, in a week or so, become my own. Shel's checkbook was already flagged at the next check.

"'Guest at the Party'"— he's got a title," Shel mused in a way that vouchsafed that John Dante was a modest, truthful man. Though he had lived in the Playboy Mansion for decades, both men invited by their great friend Hef—as Hugh Hefner was called—this friend of theirs considered himself a guest. It was Hef's house. He bought it, and he paid the bills. But the title of John Dante's book was about all that satisfied Shel that lovely spring day. After our happy waitress brought our cappuccinos and biscotti and set down our dainty napkins and cool glasses of Italian water, Shel dipped his forefinger into the sugar bowl t ticked the granules off his tongue.

"Jeez, he wants to use the proceeds from book sales to move to Florence. How could you want to spend your last years in a place where you've never been?"

View from the Ponte Vecchio, Florence.
Photo by Anthony Valerio

To the right of our small round table was a large-format photograph of the Ponte Vecchio, the old bridge in Florence. large-format photograph of Florence's Ponte Vecchio. It made sense. Spend your waning days up north in the hometown of your namesake, the poet Dante. Shel shook his great bald pate in incredulity. Beads of sweat broke out on his plethora of liver spots. He was really upset that John Dante wanted to write about his "interesting yet checkered journey…" that led him, "inexorably," to meeting Hugh Hefner, instead of the Playboy world itself that he had helped build, with its glamour, women, sex, movie stars. Otherwise, the work wouldn't sell, and his friend's wish to live out his life in Florence would end up a pipe dream.

"I mean, here's a guy who was a bartender in the first Playboy club, then Hef's Assistant, acquiring estimable power, and he comes and lives in the Playboy Mansion and, for the next 26 years, lives with, at any one given time, 40 of the most beautiful women in the world! Had his own apartment—king-size bed, kitchenette, parlor. Dial 20 for deluxe room service, champagne, caviar, anything he wanted. Ja-a-h-h-n hired thousands of indebted, gorgeous women for Bunny jobs. For the London Playboy club alone, he interviewed three thousand of the most desirable women on the British Isles in mesh stockings and high heels for 200 jobs that he alone could grant. For Christ's sake! He managed the Playboy jet, choosing and picking among the crème-de-la-crème for the stewardess jobs, and flew all over the world with them. He continued: "Do you know what John wants to write about, after living the life of a Sultan, the kind of life every bachelor fantasizes about? His teacher! He wants to write about fucking his substitute grammar school teacher, a Miss…Miss...!"

Our waitress placed our bill gingerly on the table. Shel grabbed it.

"I have to go. I have a date tonight, a rollerblader from California."

The driving force for great lovers such as Shel Silverstein and John Dante and Hugh Hefner and Rodolfo Valentino in the movies and the original Casanova de Seingalt was the next woman on the near horizon whom they could possibly love.

"She said she would call when she got in town."

"Has she?" I asked.

"What?"

"The rollerblader from California, has she called?" I reminded him.

"Not yet," Shel answered. "But you should see her."

I stand outside the chipped white fence of John Dante's bungalow in Fort Lauderdale, Florida, looking into his yard. It is a wasteland of fragmented palm and crags of sod and grass. It is also the place to which John Dante has descended. This is his contrapasso, *the punishment that suits his sins: ending in a "hellhole" while he had lived for 26 years in an elegant mansion with a Game House, swimming pool, aviary, burial ground for his beloved poodles, and the most beautiful women in the world. Inside John Dante's bungalow is exactly how Shel described it—Hell in the form of an airtight room, all the windows and doors shut, the air stifling and stale, reeking of tobacco new and old, the one ashtray a mountain of ash, the poodles reveling in their own stink. John looks old and haggard. His swarthy face is wrinkled, sagged. His full crop of black hair is disheveled, and his beard is days old. Believing that I am looking for a reason for his decline, he says, "I've had a heart attack." But then he says with some élan, "Come, I want to show you something, and gets up and leads me into the bathroom, and then points behind the door to a black and white pencil drawing on the wall. "Shel gave it to me. A guy lynched by his own dick." A long, hose-like penis, neither circumcised nor uncircumcised, extends from a guy's loins then loops up and twists around his neck, like a noose. John continued: "It was either a prediction or a warning that maybe I'd hang myself by the neck and get my ass out of there."*

We sit at his sticky, Formica-top table. In front of John Dante rises a stack of yellow legal pads filled with the clear, firm script of the Catholic schoolboy. I have brought along my mini Voice Sensor recording device and a stack of microcassettes. John drums his fingers on the table in nervous expectation. He begins to talk. I press RECORD.

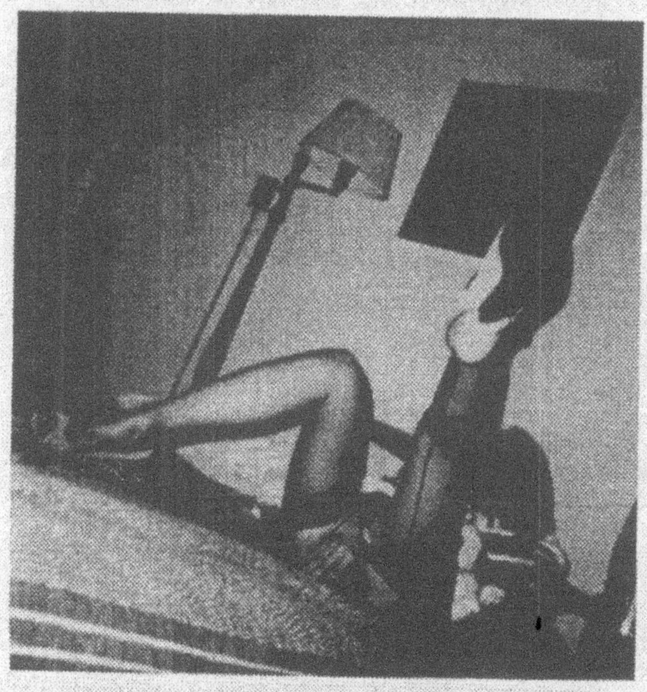

polaroid, John Dante's personal collection

1. DANTE'S INFERNO

"At a very early age I had a tremendous affinity to women, and it seems to me now in retrospect that at every decisive crossroad of my life, a woman was there to direct my path."--John Dante

"It was inevitable that I would meet Hugh Hefner. In fact, everything I did and everything that happened seemed to lead, inexorably, to meeting this fascinating, complex man."-John Dante

"ABANDON EVERY HOPE, WHO ENTER HERE."

--Dante Alighieri, *Inferno*, Canto 3

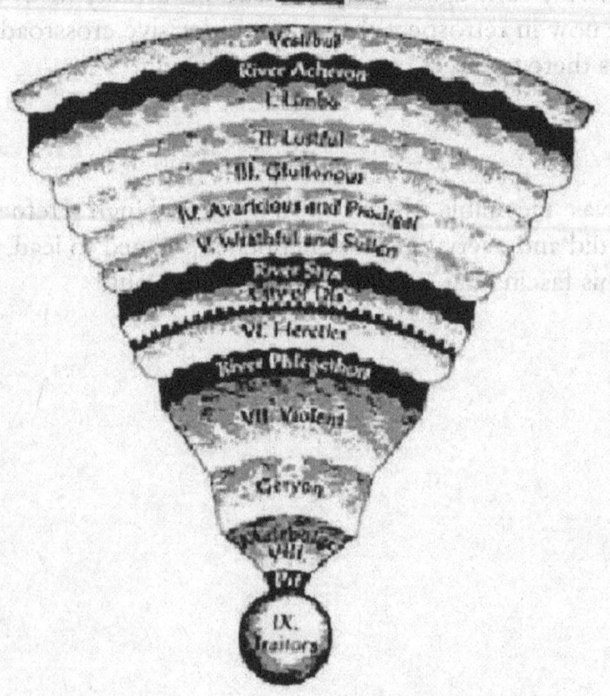

Dante Alighieri's scheme of Hell composed of Circles and Bolges, or Pits.

Matchbook Cover, Dante's Inferno

"It was some time in December 1957 and my club Dante's Inferno was about to open. I'd sent out staggered invitations to important people in town, Mayor Richard Daley and TV talk show hosts Irv Kupcinet and Marty Faye, but the one person I wanted to come was Hugh Hefner. I'd become a devotee of the magazine and had started to collect it."

For someone like him who didn't speak English until the age of eight, a picture of a beautiful, half-clad woman was worth a thousand halting words.

He'd placed a small ad in *Playboy* consisting of a Dante's Inferno's matchbook cover of a devilish red devil with a horny tail holding a pitchfork. In Dante's Inferno he had created something new and stylish and exciting in Chicago's night life out of abandonment and decay, and he wanted Hugh Hefner to see it.

Snowflakes the size of quarters fell on Chicago's Skid Row. The flames he had carved out of the rooftop would have to wait for the snow to stop and melt in order to blaze through. The red devil carved in wood outside his place was ankle high in snow. Dante's Inferno did not have an address on the front door. Game enough to experience Hell for an evening? Go down to Dante's Inferno near Skid Row.

He had Opening Night jitters. Not a soul was going to come through the front door to be greeted by a rush of warmth and the beautiful blonde hostess, Renée. Or hear the wonderful musician Frank D'Rone under one blue spotlight sing American standards. Or take in the original mahogany bar and sample the hors d'oeuvres table filled with Swedish meatballs and caviar and complimentary glass of champagne. Or see for the first time in the history of Chicago night life waitresses in mesh stockings, leotards, and high heels. Last but not least, take a complimentary excursion through Hell because hanging all around on the walls were five-foot blowups of Gustav Doré's etchings of Dante Alighieri's epic poem *Dante's Inferno,* to which the ingenious proprietor had added phosphorescent paint so that the sheer black and white chiaroscuro did not appear too stark. Small blue lights beneath each etching added subtle accents. No legends accompanied Hell's sufferers and its demon beasts and the various and sundry circles and pits of Hell--but the proprietor would gladly provide such information upon request. No one to come and see and hear growling on the rear wall the bearded, reclining Minos, King of the Underworld, supreme judge of the naked, cowering, shamed souls herded below him, his powerful tail horribly wrapping around--womp! womp!—the number of times indicating, according to your sins, the circle of your terrible, inescapable destiny. Six-thirty, seven o'clock—the place was empty. He went up to his office and stood at the window and looked out at the snow.

Renée called up. "People are coming in. Mayor Daley sent his son, and Kupcinet and Marty Faye are here."

He writes:

"It amazed me because I had built Dante's near Skid Row."

"There is no greater pain than to remember a happy time in wretchedness." Dante, *Inferno*, Canto 5, 121-122

His mother, a diminutive Italian immigrant, had feared that he might end up on Skid Row or worse, in prison or killed, along with the other Italian boys who came up around Taylor and Maxwell Streets, Chicago's Little Italy known as the "Patch," where she bought him second-hand clothes and ill-fitting shoes, and where sports such as baseball and boxing and the military and crime were ways out of their ghetto. Her Giovanni must not become a member of the "42 gang," nine year olds with dirty dark faces and knees and black greasy hair who became notorious vandals, thieves, car strippers, and robbers of horses from the stables of local fruit and produce peddlers. Their streets were the training grounds for Al Capone's and then Sam "Momo" Giancana's "Outfit." Of the original 42 gang members, more than 30 were killed, seriously wounded or imprisoned for murder, armed robbery, and sexual assault. So his mother scrimped and saved working in a hot laundry to afford to send him away to a boarding school, St. Bede's, run by Benedictine monks who flitted around in black hooded robes, their step slow, agonizing. The monks taught *The Divine Comedy* by Dante Alighieri, which tells the story of the author/pilgrim's journey to paradise and God and his muse and love, Beatrice. But, lost in error and sin, Dante must first journey through Hell, which takes from Maundy Thursday to Easter Sunday, the same amount of time, one weekend, of your average guy's entire lifetime of orgasms. One monk read the text in Italian and another flashed Frenchman's Gustav Doré's black and white, or chiaroscuro, illustrations of the *Inferno* on a pull-down screen. The classroom lights dimmed, and Johnny Aimola sat transfixed in the dark, sucked into the subterranean world of Doré's illustrations as into a cosmic comic book. There were woods with talking, bleeding trees, the threatening She-Wolf with yellow eyes, bolts of lightning raining down and tearing into the Sodomites' naked bodies, Murderers up to their eyes in the River of Blood. Every kind of sinner you could think of was down there--the lustful, the thieves, the hypocrites, the fraudulent, the betrayers of community—suffering, naked shades who could still feel pain, howling like dogs. The Chiaroscuro style made so much sense. Black and white was the color of his parents' world of the Great Depression, of their walk-up flat with peeling walls, of the men and women in black and white rags pounding Chicago's unforgiving pavement in search of a black and white job, hoping against hope to find one that paid 10 cents a day. Waiting on long lines for a black and white apple. For these people back home, there was no beatific glow of the sun, for the sun was black and it was silent.

The monk was saying:

"…*contrapasso* is Dante's scheme of sin-punishment. Suffer according to the nature of your sin. For example, John Aimola, if you don't pay attention, you will be struck deaf and dumb."

He is 13 years old and sits in class two weeks before grammar school graduation. Hitler has invaded Poland and Italy has invaded Ethiopia, and the Italian immigrant fathers are nervous. Having survived America's Great Depression, with a World War so close upon its heels, they suffer the bitter irony of their homeland fighting against America, land of their dreams. Instead of his nun teacher with her chiaroscuro black veil enveloping her white habit and giant black rosary beads wrapping around her white narrow waist and trailing down her white habit along her lanky, hidden, fair thigh—a lay teacher strides into the classroom. The sun begins to sing.

This is the substitute grammar school teacher Shel Silverstein was so upset about, the one his friend insisted on writing about.

"Good morning, boys and girls--"and she turns and writes her name on the board—"my name is Susan Einway, and I will be your teacher till the end of the term."

For little Johnny Aimola, it was like all the chiaroscuro in the world suddenly turned bright yellows and reds. His crop of black hair, followed by his black eyes, rose ever so slightly above the still, uniform heads of his classmates.

"She wore silk blouses and always smelled wonderful. She'd come in wearing a jacket, but then she'd take it off. She had pretty, pretty legs. The seams of her stockings were straight as arrows. A brunette with a mole one-half inch from her lip. I got a tickle in my groin. It was lust, sheer lust, and she felt it."

Miss Einway says, "Mr. Aimola, why don't you come forward to this seat up front. Your name begins with an 'A,' does it not?"

He moves up to the second seat. Miss Einway's habit was to lecture with "her ass on the first desk, her feet on the front of my desk. My eyes glued to her knees, hoping she would open them."

On the last Friday before the long, hot summer, she keeps him after class on some presumption.

"Who do you like to play with, John?"

"Theresa and Vaughn," he answered.

"And what do you do?'

"Play games. Kissing games."

"Really? Who do you like?"

"Theresa Mineo."

"Do you kiss Theresa a lot? How do you kiss?"

With that, he leans forward, opens his mouth, and projects a bit of his tongue.

"She sucked my tongue into her mouth." He draws back slightly and sees the fair skin of her face flush crimson. Then—"I put my hand on her tits. I was 13 and she was 25, 26."

"Wait--" and she gets up and takes him by the hand and presses a button on one of the four blackboards, which then raise and rumble, like thunder. Hidden behind these magical boards was the clothes closet. Because it was spring, there was plenty of room.

"She starts grabbing me, playing with me. She gets down on her knees and sucks."

Thus, John Aimola, a.k.a. John Dante, began his one weekend of ecstatic bliss.

"Promise not to tell anyone," she tells him afterward.

"Promise," he says, which is like telling the priest in the confessional that, over the next week, he will not commit another sin. But he kept his promise, at least then. Not that he didn't want to tell his best friend, Dominick. And not that it wasn't the greatest thing that could ever happen to the two of them. But because, even if he tried, he would not have been able to find the words.

"Strike it Rich! Gold in the Valley of the Headless Men! "

In order to position himself in the proximity of beautiful women like Susan Einway and make love to them, he first had to get rich. He saw it in *Sir* magazine, which he read at his desk at St. Bede's, and he saw it in the movies.

"They're the guys, good or bad, with the penthouses and the ladies."

So he got hold of a plastic pan, shovel, trowel, and magnate and, knapsack over his shoulder, ran away from St Bede's and headed out to the Northwest Territories to pan for gold. He staked a claim at the foot of the Franklin Mountains, sifting the ankle-high sediment in his stream. Mud. Stones. Not a nugget.

"That didn't pan out and I came back to Chicago."

But he could not have struck a mother lode and mined it and become rich, because then he would have had the wherewithal to buy his own mansion and to gather to himself his own harem, and his checkered, interesting journey would not have lead him, inexorably, to meeting Hugh Hefner. But another get-rich scheme had presented itself right away, one as natural to John Aimola as pasta and baccala—crime. In those days, anything out of the norm, call John. His old friend Petey Antoni called.

"John, this friend, a truck driver, just stopped by and left a large carton. A dozen Hart Shaffner & Marx suits from Koppenheimer's."

Koppenheimer's was the 1950s equivalent of today's Nicholas Joseph Custom tailors. Upon finishing his route, this truck driver friend found one extra carton that had been loaded inadvertently.

"Hey, you interested in buying some nice suits?" asked the truck driver. "I got twelve silk suits here."

Petey contacted him because John Dante knew about finance and well-dressed men.

"Give him a low-ball figure, he'll probably take it," John advised, which is what happened.

"We each took one suit and sold the others for a profit."

News traveled around the west side like wild fire. Other truck drivers started stealing nice suits and bringing them to John and Petey. Soon--

"Petey and I had one of the biggest fencing operations in town. We operated out of Cicero, Illinois."

He was 19 years old and was making $3,000 per week. The year was 1947. He had bypassed Skid Row and was still breathing.

John Dante, Acapulco, Mexico. Courtesy John Dante, private collection

The romance of the Italian gangster a la John Dante continued on with his getting busted for his fencing operation in Cicero, Illinois, while conducting a major love affair with one Katherine Alyne Foster, in the sunny clime of Acapulco, Mexico. Kate was formerly from New York, where she had been married to a publisher, and so John Aimola cavorted with a woman who had been loved by a successful man of letters.

"She was probably the only woman I ever loved."

"Probably," because for a man such as himself who had aroused the affection of thousands of the prime ladies, the difference between affection and caring and love is a hair's-breadth. Though raised in a cold, windy city, he carried the bright, warm sun of southern Italy in his bones and so on vacations and when he was on the lam, he escaped to New Mexico and Acapulco. He could meet probably the only woman he ever loved only in a place where the sun sang and lemons were bright yellow and the size of grapefruits, where he could park his powder blue Cadillac on a promontory overlooking Acapulco Bay and have the beautiful, statuesque, blonde Kate Forster smelling divine of Je Reviens move over under his arm. As they danced at Coletta's morning bar, the new day's sun rose.

Thus far, his history had produced a rough-cut Italian diamond. It would take probably the only woman he ever loved to smooth the coarse edges and elevate the standard Italian 21 carats to the American 24.

"Kate refined this Italian street kid. She was a very classy lady, 15 years older, haughty, beautiful blonde, great figure, kind of a W.A.S.P. that, when you're in high school, you see these beautiful blondes and think, 'They're out of my realm.' "

Would they see one another up in Chicago?

His crime partner Petey's wife knew where to reach him in Acapulco, and she was alarmed.

"Petey got nailed by the F.B.I. so you gotta get back because it's going to cost money to take care of."

He returned to Chicago and paid their way out, Petey's and his, in exactly what corrupt manner John does not say. Shel knew about John's association with the Chicago gangsters, he'd seen how they interacted in the Playboy clubs and in the Mansion and that, in all likelihood, John had access to Chicago's corrupt politicians. His path had crossed with Willie "Ice" Atorino's in Cicero, Illinois, as Outfit boss Momo Giancana had consigned to Mr. Atorino the responsibility of knowing every thief in Chicago so that the Outfit could excise a "Street Tax", or "Tribute", in return for protection and continued good health—kind of like paying an insurance premium. Everybody in Chicago knew Ice's reputation for the tortuous slow kill, using a prelude of ice picks and blowtorches. If there was tribute to pay, everybody also knew, you paid it. John Dante did not necessarily have to be a convicted felon or a jailbird to have his path lead, inexorably, to Hugh Hefner, but if he had continued on with his criminal career, like the majority of Outfit members, he probably would have gotten himself killed. In that case, he would have had to meet up with Hef in Paradise.

Momentarily, he wanted to stay with Katherine Forster, who *did* want to see him up in Chicago. Feeling like he had a fresh start after paying his way out, though he'd had to sell his horse and his plane in which he'd been logging in flight hours so that he could have access to all of the world's warm, bright spots--he didn't know how to be with Kate up in Chicago. Dancing a foxtrot intoxicated by Je Reviens perfume at Coletta's morning bar bathed in the new day's golden rays was one thing, but back on his stomping grounds in bleak black and white Chicago with Petey and Tony and Luigi and the gangsters was quite another. But there was as much of the Italian in him in Chicago as there had been in Acapulco so he took Kate to Luigi's Pizzeria for "pasta and all that jazz." He had named his dog after Luigi, certainly he could take a date to his place. Kate seemed to enjoy it. She allowed him to be who he was and, at the same time, let him in. All was well with the red, green, and white Italian world. After the drive to her home in a fancy neighborhood of single-family houses with lawns and trees, he double-parked out front and mused: should I tell her? Hell, why not?

"Kate, I'd like to fuck you in the worst way."

A pregnant pause--teetering at the edge of one of Hell's precipices. Then

"Why in the worst way?" she said right away. "Why not fuck me in the best way. Go park your car and ring my bell."

Katherine Forster fucked him in the best way for four straight days and, during brief respites, chose, in these best of times in her young Italian lover's life, to fine-tune him. With her satin sheet drawn up, her hair spilling gold over her shoulders onto their pillow, she called the Embers.

"Two steaks medium rare…bottle of Brut. Merci."

John may have told his closest friends including Shel Silverstein and Hugh Hefner that, on the subject of finding a soul mate among all the beautiful women who entered their lives--Bunnies, Playmates, models, actresses--it was Katherine Forster, a woman all of her own, who had prepared him to know the best that other men could ever hope for. So that he could experience his fine tuning first hand, they got out of bed, and she took him to the Embers, the Pump Room, and the Café de Paris. She ordered Beluga caviar and champagne and, when they finished a bottle, she set it neck down in the bucket, signaling for a fresh one. She took him to Marshal Fields and picked out of few outfits for herself, and took him into her dressing room so that he could watch her try on clothes that he liked to see her in. Then—the coup de grace! Kate taught him perhaps the greatest lesson of all, liberation from the conventional two-to-tango to the sharing of love and lust—communal sex, the ménage à trois, the orgy. Kate invited her friend Jean to stop by on her way to the Indianapolis speedway, and she stayed two weeks. Fourteen days and nights of gorgeous women making love to him at the same time, and he to them, wherein he knew full well that, when he was being kissed and when he was being sucked off, it was by a woman. He took off one night to shoot crap in Pino's basement. Shel Silverstein may have known about John and the Chicago gangsters and that my Uncle Tommy was a driver for one Charles "Lucky" Luciano, that when the two boys were growing up on the Lower East Side of Manhattan and Uncle Tommy's new watch was stolen and his mother went and pleaded with Charlie Lucky's mother and the next day a stranger walked up to Tommy and handed him his watch and that, when I was a boy looking out my mother's window on a wintry afternoon, I saw a camel's hair coat for the first time, worn by Mr. Luciano, who was pacing in front of my house, coattails flying, brown fedora pulled down low on his hard, square forehead, waiting for his girlfriend to finish with the dentist—but none of us, Shel or Petey or my Uncle Tommy ever shot craps with Outfit boss Salvatore "Momo" Giancana. For down into Pino's basement walks Giancana with a navy blue cashmere coat draped over his shoulders, flanked by two square men.

"He walks up to the table and says, 'Shoot a nickel,' and throws down five $100 bills, and then turns to shoot the breeze because he knows it'll take ten or fifteen minutes for the fucking guys to fade him. But I'm looking at his coat—wow, is that gorgeous!"

Shooting the breeze because most of the fucking guys worked for him, all the while thinking, Here's one of our own who made it big, going from wheel man to capo regime to national—no global!—fame, meshing the mafia and political machines first to get J.F.K. elected, then get him killed, then work with the C.I.A. on assassinating Cuban dictator Fidel Castro. Choosing between being intimidated by a notorious gangster from the same neighborhood or admiring a rare stylish coat, John Aimola opted for the coat. Anybody could shoot crap or wind up on Skid Row or become a gangster, but not anybody could wear a navy blue cashmere coat while sitting behind the wheel of a powder blue Cadillac. That night, he faded Momo Giancana to the tune of $1,400, and lost. Normally, he would settle markers at the end of the week but not this marker, the one owed to Momo Giancana on the night he shot crap with him, because by the weekend there would have been etched on his tombstone not words or his real or adopted name but an image carved in stone of a young, dark-skinned Italian fellow with wild black wavy hair sitting in a powder blue Cadillac, looking back over his shoulder at a woman in seamed stockings and high heels. He wrote a check (which later bounced) for the debt and paid off in cash. He rushed home and told Kate Forster, whom he could not take to Pino's basement, but she and W.A.S.P.s in general knew about Momo and his sunglasses and fancy dress. Poste-haste, she took him out and bought him the same navy blue cashmere coat.

One day soon after, the cashmere coat hanging in the closet and the Cadillac parked outside, Kate said:

"I'm pregnant--"his fertile seed, a masculine child to carry on the Aimola name—"Let's get married."

Married?

"The thought never entered my mind."

By his nature, lust superseded fidelity, so he would certainly wind up in Hell's Circle 5, hurricane winds tossing, wheeling, prodding him now here, now there, moaning, lamenting along with the other Adulterers.

"Kate went to Acapulco to have the baby, miscarried, and married her doctor."

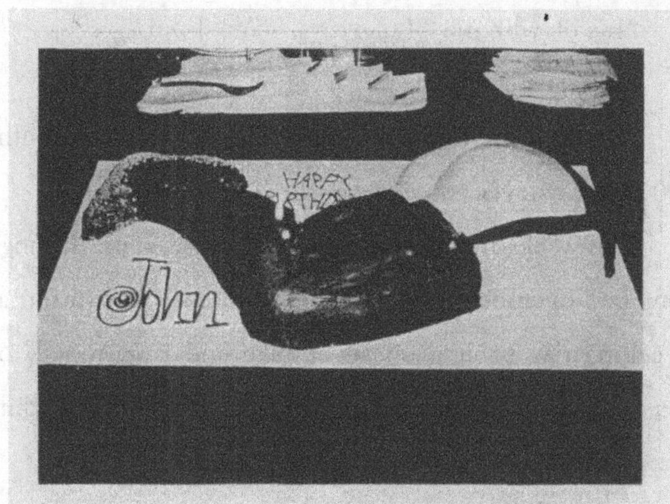

Courtesy John Dante, private collection

The direct path from John Aimola to becoming John Dante and the inexorability of his decisions that lead him to meeting Hugh Hefner began, of course, with a woman and, at his present crossroad, it was Frankie from New Orleans. With his heart heavy over the one woman he probably loved in the arms of her gynecologist in Acapulco, he took a bartender's job at Luigi's pizzeria, and one night in walks Frankie.

"She was married to a politician who, before he got thrown in jail, bought her a concession in northern Illinois, a cathouse called the Welcome Inn."

Frankie sits at the bar and sizes up the bartender--around 30 years old, mop of riotous black wavy hair, bulbous nose, high wide forehead like something's going on in there. Luigi ambles over. Says Frankie, pointing:

"Can I borrow him for a month? I have to take care of my mother and need a manager up at the inn."

"It's ok with me," Luigi says. "Ask John."

She leans forward:

"Look, John, I've got to have $35,000 for the month. I'll give you $3,000 and, whatever you make at the bar, you keep."

The Welcome Inn had two high seasons: fishing in July and hunting in November. Sweating anglers in need of comfort and relaxation after a long day hauling up silver pike and large-mouth bass. Freezing hunters exhausted from tracking, killing, and skinning white-tail deer. It was late October, onset of the hunting season.

Sunlight dappled through the firs and junipers of north Wisconsin's lake district, as the powder blue Cadillac followed an off-roar spur, not quite a gravel road, to the Welcome Inn, which had a huge parking lot and a barn. He slowly pulled the Caddie into the barn.

The house had a small bar with ten stools that lead into a parlor, where the girls sat. Each girl, five in all, had her own separate room to work in, one woman took care of the house year round, and one prostitute worked the off-season to serve your occasional widower, poacher, adventurous hiker. Two days before Opening Day, Big Helen, Red, and Candy arrived, along with two other prostitutes, who, coming in from the busy country fair circuit, found warmth and a roof over their heads.

Opening night arrived and he got the jitters. 9 p.m. He looked outside. Not a soul. Big Helen and Candy sauntered over and tapped his ass.

"Don't worry about it," they reassured him.

Now the clock read 10 p.m.

"The whole fucking parking lot was filled—exhausts running, a cloud of smoke over the whole place."

Frankie had told him to sell drinks for $.50 a piece.

"I charged a dollar and the men waiting their turn were three deep at the bar."

The girls gave him $1,200 per day to put aside for Frankie and, delighted by the respectful way he treated them, gave him a $1,000 gift and for his birthday, November 20, woolen pleated shirts from Pendleton Mills. One girl, a first timer, had taken a liking to him and gave him a watch.

Driving back to Chicago along the barren woods, he said to himself:

"This is the business to be in. I'll open a small, inconspicuous cathouse and in a year 'll make enough money to open a legit club on Rush Street."

But prostitution was not an option, the Chicago gangsters soon informed him—still, not knowing a thing about the nightclub business, he found himself cruising Rush Street for "to let" signs late into the night which brought with it a blanketing silence. Knowledge or the lack of it of the nightclub business, parents, gangsters, failed love affairs—none of that seemed to matter now. He had to find a location. Rents on Rush Street were too expensive. Save for one fewer moment of searching, Johnny Aimola would not have become John Dante and he and Hef might never have met. He was turning the wheel in the direction back to the west side when he spotted a small, two-storey, frame house with two large plate-glass windows. He pulled over, got out and went over and pressed his face against the glass. The window was so murky that he couldn't see his reflection. His hellish shade had appeared even before his transformation to John Dante. Cupping his hands above his eyes, through a crack in the grime he saw "a dark, filthy room, filled with junk." His curiosity was pricked. "Where am I?...Huron Street…OK…in the middle of the block between Deerborn and Clark…wait a minute, Deerborn and Clark are in the middle of Skid Row!" In the blackness and silence of night, he walked the half block to Clark Street. Derelicts and drunks and lost souls lay across doorways, and staggered. Still others "huddled in doorways in the fetal position, temporarily escaping their misery through the luxury of sleep." Blue, yellow, and red lights flashed on and off at the top of the block. He walked up there, then turned onto Clark Street. Saloons beckoning easy prey in neon light—a shot of whiskey and a beer for 15 cents—lined both sides of the street. He glanced up—the intense lights diffused almost completely as they reached second-story flophouses with dirty windows, where you could get a bed for 50 cents. He counted five cheap strip joints and a dozen or so pawnshops in that two-block stretch. Derelicts approached him, hands out, mumbling incoherently.

He walked back to his car, settled in, and sat in the darkness. He looked over at the small, abandoned framed building. This was it. He would build his club here. He pictured "Dante's Inferno" up in black and white lights. He would compete for Chicago's night life in a legitimate way, by default, so to speak. Besides, if he had gone ahead with a house of prostitution, most likely he would not have met Hugh Hefner. Time was vaulting in his favor.

"OK, I'll cater to the people of Chicago on the premise of going slumming. In other words, go to Skid Row to this sharp little place." He would open a first-class club whose motif was consistent with life on nearby Skid Row--Hell.

"I built the whole fucking place myself. Two carpenter friends of Luigi's showed me how to hold a hammer and use a plumb bob. I got up on the roof with a chainsaw and cut it into flames and panted it red. I cut a red devil into the façade and painted that red. I went to ceramics school and then built the bar out of red mosaic tiles with a black bat composed mainly of wings in the center." Chicago's Skid Row had a few new infernal wrinkles. "I also made the ashtrays."

One day, this patrol car passes by, and two cops see a powder blue Cadillac and some guy in overalls up on the roof carving flames with a chainsaw.

"What's going on?" one cop calls up.

"Opening a small nightclub."

"Have you checked with Captain Hannigan?"

"Captain Hannigan? No."

"Jesus Christ, you better check it out with the captain because you're going to need him for your liquor license."

"Really," he feigned surprise. "I thought I'd go to City Hall and get my liquor license."

"No, that's not how it works."

So he went to see Captain Hannigan, who said:

"Have you talked to the Monk?"

"Monk…?" Was he back at St. Bede's?

"Get the fuck out of here!" the captain yelled at him. He left with a smile because he knew that the admonition signaled a payoff along the way to acquiring his liquor license. He spoke to his friend Billy, who owned the Rainbow Room:

"Go see Hannigan again and this time bring a priest."

A priest was the go-between between him and Monk. A man of God was the go-between between corrupt Chicago and the city's major gangsters. It made a kind of sense. It was like confessing your sins--in order to attain salvation, first you had to sin.

The second time he met with Hannigan, he brought a priest. A meeting was finally arranged with Monk Leonetti.

The Monk held court round midnight in his restaurant, Valentino's, named after the matinee idol Rodolfo Valentino, known as The Great Lover, an Italian immigrant from the same Puglia region as John Aimola. At 12:30, Davey the doorman ushered John to the Monk's corner table. Little did Monk Leonetti know that the man who just sat down opposite him would soon become a real-life Great Lover. Bald, stocky, hunched over, the Monk—

"So you're the kid opening the little joint down the street?"

Red spots on his tie indicated the chef's special of marinara sauce.

"Yes. A small private club," he responded.

"I heard about it. Flames, devil—real hell, huh? What's it going to be, a fag joint?"

Making it a gay club had not occurred to him. Besides, his prospective business partner, Darlene, "a good-looking Polish woman from the neighborhood," had fallen in love with the lesbian who was going to design Dante's. Even before Dante's Inferno opened, Darlene was headed for Circle 6 Bolge 9.

"OK, kid, go ahead. Buy the liquor from the boys and nobody 'll bother you."

Frank D'Rone, Circa 1960. Dante's Inferno

Around 8 o'clock, Renée called up:

"Hugh Hefner just came in."

He was still upstairs in his office. "You have got to be kidding."

"No. He's here with another guy."

So he went down and saw and heard the buzz of Dante's Inferno's first customers' eyes and mouths wide open, looking and pointing at Gustav Doré's scenes of Hell from banquettes and chairs of all sizes. The bar was hopping, and Frank D'Rone was playing and singing under one spotlight. Though *Playboy* magazine was already a big success, Hugh Hefner's visage was not as yet well known.

"Two guys stood together, one wearing an elegant black mohair suit and the other in penny loafers and white socks and a kind of Brooks Brothers jacket and maybe a cardigan sweater."

The tallish guy in the mohair suit looked the part of a playboy so he extended his hand to the one whom he believed was Hugh Hefner. Then he said it for the first time:

"Hi, I'm John Dante."

He had signed the invitations Johnny Dante to go along with the place.

"It made sense promotionally because if I had signed them 'John Aimola,' people would have said, 'Who the fuck is John Aimola?' I'm reinventing myself." He was not thinking exactly of his great forefather Dante Alighieri. "I was thinking of Humphrey Bogart who is Ricky Blaine in the film *Casablanca.* I was picturing myself this kind of entrepreneur." He saw himself as the savvy, cynical American expatriate owner of an upscale night spot and illegal gambling den, Rick's Café Américain, as a Humphrey Bogart/Ricky Blaine whose heart was broken by a beautiful woman in Paris which they would always have—Bogey and Ingrid Bergman/Elsa Lazlo, who was married to a famous Czech freedom fighter and into whose arms, in the end, patriotism superseding romantic love, Ricky delivers his loved one. Finally, John Aimola had become John Dante, and he had extended his hand to the wrong man, Victor Lownes, who shook it nonetheless and said:

"No, this is Hugh Hefner."

John Dante turned and looked into Hugh Hefner's face for the first time. He was "thin, almost emaciated, and I saw an integrity, a forthrightness, an honesty. He looked straight at you when he spoke." He extended his hand to the right guy and said again, confirming his transformation from an ordinary Italian to one with a famous name and name of his classy establishment—

"Hi, I'm John Dante."

Gambling and women—they had started together with this reversible, forever linked, tandem. The Gaslight Club, like Dante's Inferno, predated the Playboy Club, and he was going with a Gaslight girl, and friends Shelley and Skippy had their girls, and Hef his, and they were all swinging. A singer at the Cloister Inn, Billie Nelson, "good-looking, with big tits"—they all boffed her.

"The girls were treated as chattel. They belonged to us. There may have been a bit of honor where you couldn't fuck around with somebody else's girlfriend, but that was ignored, too."

Around this time, he revised his first impression of Hef as unworldly and ill at ease with women.

"He asked me for the name of a hooker. In turn, I asked him about a knockout, platinum blonde, a Jean Harlow look-alike. 'She's due to come in the following week,' Hef told me."

Discreet and modest, John does not say whether he had directed the aforementioned hooker Hef's way, but he does recollect the knockout Jean Harlow double.

"The following week, Renée called up:

"'Hef is here with a good-looking blonde.'

"I was shaving and cut myself and went downstairs, forgetting about the pieces of toilet tissue stuck to my face. Hef looks at my face and says, 'What happened?' "

Dante's Inferno was up and running in a successful, legitimate way and had begun to rival the Cloister Inn as far as the talent it attracted. Talented Frank D'Rone brought in the great Ella Fitzgerald. Nat King Cole came and sat at the small, out-of-tune spinet that nobody used and played it divinely as accompaniment to Frank D'Rone's singing. Cole would write the liner notes to D'Rone's album, *Frank D'Rone Sings:*

"A singer with an individual sound that invites no comparisons. A singer who can seemingly sustain a note forever; one of the few singers who can change a mood of a room from song to song by moving from one emotion to another."

John Dante was gaining notoriety as an innovative entrepreneur, and he became friends of a lifetime with Hugh Hefner, Lenny Bruce, Bob Gibson, Shel Silverstein, and Don Adams, who had won an Arthur Godfrey's Talent Show as a stand-up comic and was appearing at the Cloister Inn, owned by John's friends, Shelley and Skippy, who had discovered this funny, fouled-mouth comedian, Lenny Bruce, at the Hungry Eye in San Francisco, and brought him to Chicago. John Dante caught another unique performer.

"Shel had a ventriloquist act at the Gate of Horn."

Growing up in Chicago's Jewish neighborhood, listening to Russian, Hebrew, and Yiddish, Sheldon Allan Silverstein aspired to create dummies and throw myriad voices into them.

With 15 or 20 copies of *Playboy* tucked under his arm, Hef went around to the clubs on Rush Street and around the corner to Dante's Inferno and left a few copies. Dante's Inferno had a two o'clock license and so, after closing, the friends headed over to the Cloister Inn, located in the basement of the Maryland Hotel, which had a four o'clock license.

Then over to Milano's for coffees and warm cheese and fruit pastries. Other early mornings, the friends went over to the Tradewinds, where they had their own table. Across the room sitting at their exclusive table was a different group of night owls, quiet, intoning a few words in Sicilian dialect that only Johnny Dante, although of Calabrese extraction, well understood, for they'd all been immigrants from the same streets in Chicago's Little Italy. There they were, members of the Outfit—"Sheriff" Matolla, Joe "Nose" Taura, Willie "Ice" Atorino.

"They knew us. They waved and called over, 'Hiya, Don…Art…Lenny…Shel. How ya doin', John?' "

One night, he and Tony Roma walk into Diamond Jim Moran's and slide into a banquette, followed by Carlos Silva—"a brutal outfit guy from Kansas City"—and his wife, who sits next to this swarthy Italian who owns and operates a club of his own with Hell as its theme. Her eyes widen because sleeping with a gangster is one thing, but getting to know one who has created his own Hell on earth is quite another. Nevertheless, this Dante is all smiles and smooth, working on a dish of oysters surrounding a small cup of vodka. Suddenly, he feels something land on his thigh. He doesn't have to look down to see whose hand it is.

"Hey, stop by my club," he says to everybody as he was leaving, and passes around a couple of Dante's Inferno's matchbooks with a cover of a flaming Beelzebub holding a pitchfork.

Gustav Doré, Paolo and Francesca. Dante's Inferno.

Mrs. Silva stopped by, alone, before Dante's opened. She pointed to the blown-up, lit Gustav Doré etching of a couple bathing in the brightness of their chiaroscuro, blown hither and yon by a black wind, enveloped in a cocoon by a rustling sheet shaped like an empty oyster shell. He was already in Hell, but he wanted Mrs. Silva to know what was in store for an adulterer if she continued up to his private office. How the adulterers Francesca da Rimini and her Paolo suffered down in Hell's Circle 2. Hell was reaching back over your shoulder and feeling your lover's nose and eyes but unable to turn and see him or her. Hell was telling your sad story in Hell to a pilgrim who still has a chance to reach Paradise, while your illicit lover behind you weeps. Hell on earth was Francesca da Rimini trying to protect her lover from her jealous, raging husband and getting run through by his thrusting knife, dying in a swoon in her lover's arms, and then having him run through, too. If he found out, Carlos Silva would kill her, and then she would come face to face with the growling beast King Minos gnashing his teeth, and he would snap and wrap his tail around her twice—womp! womp!—and send her, forever, down to Circle 2. Nevertheless, Mrs. Silva followed him up to his office, for an afternoon making love to John Dante was worth all the pains of Hell.

He survived this tryst and would go on to such popularity that he became the lover of two other gangsters' women. He had not emerged unscathed from these perilous affairs purely by happenstance or aided by his lovers' discretion and wiles. These most dangerous of Chicago's—the nation's!—gangsters knew about John Dante before they exposed their women to him, about his innate penchant for the quick turnover, that he was a man much like themselves, same upbringing, same mores, an Italian like them for whom wanton sex with all classifications of women except mothers and wives was temporary, cursory, like visiting an out-of-the-way inn and leaving the following morning, never to return. But by some quirk of nature, this John Dante was one Italian for whom marriage and family never came to mind. This guy was a real-life Casanova, a Rodolfo Valentino with a healthy libido. The gangsters reached an accord--direct their women straight into the arms of this weird paisan with whom they had no future. He could serve as a kind of airtight insurance policy or erstwhile babysitter, a transient plaything of sorts while they, the husbands, were out of town. Consorting with him would curtail amorous adventures with eligible guys. So what if their women fooled around a little, as long as they came home.

But then, one wintry night Hot Dog Lasciandrella walks into Dante's Inferno and tosses $20 on the bar.

"Hey, kid, I wanna talk to you," he says.

"What's up, Hot Dog?" He had acquired the nickname from all the frankfurters he devoured at Comiskey Park and Wrigley Field. He responded to Hot Dog, didn't take it as a put down.

"Hookers in your joint. They'll meet guys here and take them out. You make yourself five, six hundred extra a week."

"I don't think so but let me think about it."

"OK, you think about it," Hot Dog said, and left.

A couple of weeks passed, and he was up in his office when Hot Dog came in and Renée sent him up. He had a German shepherd who jumped out and pinned Hot Dog against the wall.

"Get this fucken dog off before I blow him away!"

"Luigi, come here…"

Hot Dog calmed down. "You think about what I told you?"

It was not a bordello from the beginning and should not become one now, and he had talked to Shelley and Skippy, who told him not to touch the Dog, he wasn't really connected.

"I'm pretty sure I don't want to."

"OK, kid," and the big man left.

A couple of weeks later on an early Sunday morning after a busy Saturday night, the smell of smoke penetrated his sleep, and he awoke, coughing.

"The whole front staircase was on fire."

He barely had time to slip on khakis and flip-flops before he burst down through the flames and out into the street. Somebody handed him a jacket. The sirens grew louder and louder as fire engines approached the bowels of Chicago. He went across the street to Mike's for breakfast. The small wooden stage on which Frank D'Rone performed burned and melted. The mahogany of the bar and its mosaic tiles with a red bat designed into it burst into flames. One by one, the walls with blown-up Gustav Doré's etchings caught fire and burned. Murderers in the River of Blood, the Sodomites with bolts of fire tearing into their skin, the tossed adulterous lovers Francesca and Paolo, the Pharisee Cephaisis who was crucified like Christ for sowing discord within the family, even Lucifer himself with his four sets of wings and four masticating mouths—all were made equal in the conflagration, reduced to ashes.

Then somebody called out:

"Hey, your place is on fire again!"

A second engine company arrived, and fresh firemen in heavy leather and yellow hats carrying hoses and axes rushed into Dante's Inferno. What was his *contrapasso* now, his sin, his punishment symbolized by this second fire, this complete razing to the ground? One fireman on his way in grabbed Dante's Inferno's welcome sign and tossed it inside so that it could burn, too, otherwise a red devil carved in wood standing alone on the sidewalk would look strange, out of context. Furious flames matched furious firefighters wielding hoses and axes on a singular chair and the burning, bald, homosexual Bruno Latini still up on a wall—"Aiee! Aarrg!"—he could hear Brunetto's shouts all the way from across the street in Mike's. A fireman took a last blow of his ax to a Coward who, up in the light, had sat on the proverbial fence and was neither here nor there, positioned outside Hell's gate but before the river Acheron. Well, nobody could say that John Dante was a coward. Two fires, he had refused Hot Dog twice. Getting out of the Italian ghetto would take more than one strenuous effort. Rising to his top-most level would require a second Herculean effort. But whatever anybody might say about him, now and forever, one thing was certain, and for this he became well known—

Twice John Dante refused to traffic in prostitution.

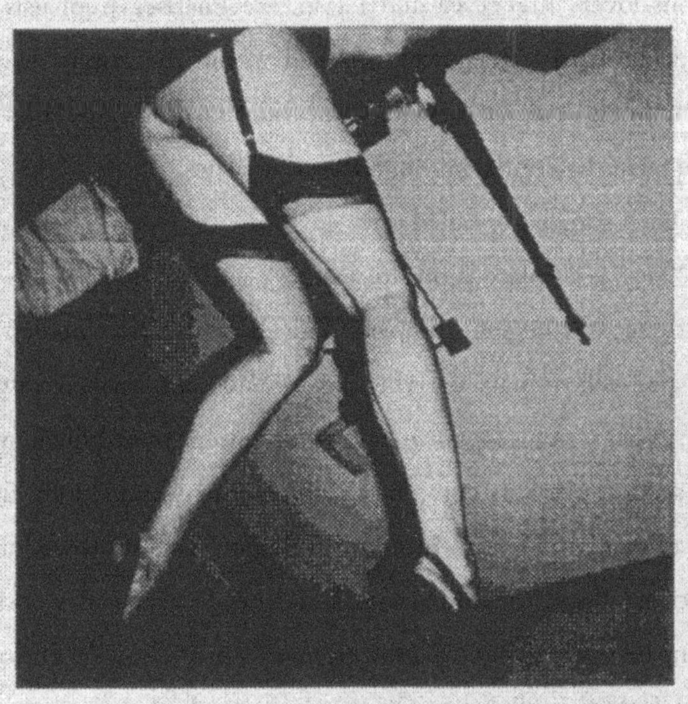

Courtesy John Dante, private collection

2. PLAYBOY

"Had the devil come up to me and said: 'Look, you want to live like a millionaire among women who are all 10's, who are hand-picked, who have gone through a gauntlet of various people before they were selected?'

"I'd have said: 'Don't even tell me what the consequences are. I don't want to know. I'm signing, I'm signing carte-blanche. I'll worry about the consequences later.' " --John Dante

After Dante's Inferno burned down twice, he did not change his name back to John Aimola, but he went into seclusion. One night during this time, Frank D'Rone hails a cab and John Dante is the driver. Frank was appalled. "Wait here," he says, and runs back up to Shelley Kasten's, and the next thing John Aimola knew, he was pulling up in front of Hugh Hefner's office at 20 Ohio Street. Remembering John Dante's classy Dante's Inferno, Hef gave him a bartender's job at the first Playboy club, located at 116 E. Walton in downtown Chicago.

Guys stood shoulder to shoulder, four deep at the bar, amid these gorgeous women in costume, 80, 90 Bunnies, all "10's". He saw the allure of the women reflected in the men's eyes. This is the kind of thing Shel wanted him to write about, as well as the close presence of the dozens upon dozens of beautiful, scantily-clad women, all milling about on shapely legs and proud bosoms, smiling. About the feelings and impressions of a man who loved women at a very early age to suddenly be working amongst the very first Playboy Bunnies. What does a man feel once he has achieved his lifetime goal of always being in the proximity of the prime ladies with the opportunity to make love to each and every one of them? If he had made love to one or to a hundred or to thousands, like Casanova de Seingalt before him, what was there about this one special Bunny as opposed to that one, or the one special prostitute among the others who had taken a liking to him at the Welcome Inn and had given him a watch for his birthday? Was this what Shel had in mind when he asked, "Has a woman ever told you what she feels when she comes?" What the 16,000 women John Dante had made love to uttered at the exact moment of their cresting sexual ecstasy, that pin-point, prick-point summit, that explosion of every sinew, the slow, long ooze, and its voiced expression? John's expertise in the nightclub business which he should also write about comes down from Frank D'Rone—"brilliant"—and then, twenty years later, from master chef and restaurateur Noel Cunningham, who was John's chef at his Touch Club of Beverly Hills—"a genius". He rose quickly from bartender to day manager to night manager—and loved every minute of it. He said as much to himself: "Fuck, I love this. I love being in the proximity of these women." He began to acquire power at a time when Hef made two decisions that involved family: purchasing a 70-room French brick and limestone mansion located at 1340 North State Parkway, on Chicago's Gold Coast, a majestic creation of the turn of the century which would serve as a residence and a workplace and also provide comfortable quarters for guests and friends; and inviting his younger brother, Keith, to become the Playboy Club's floor manager. Keith moved into "a very nice apartment in the Mansion. We became friends."

With his brother Hef closeted for days on end composing his Playboy Philosophy, Keith invited John home to play games. They played pinball and tilted and laughed. Billiard balls kissed and pocketed. At first, his movements were restricted to the Game Room, but then Hef began to throw parties. Playboy personnel were invited.

"They were like nothing I'd ever seen before."

Courtesy John Dante, private collection

At the age of 13, he had looked down upon the crown of Susan Einway fellating him, at the age of 20 had danced a foxtrot overlooking Acapulco Bay with a beautiful wealthy blonde woman who fucked him in the best way, and he had made love to three women of brutal gangsters who knew where he lived—still, he had never seen anything like the parties Hef began to throw. Playboy Bunnies and Playmates in party attire and aspiring actresses and statuesque models sent over by the agencies in the hope of catching an influential eye—all having a good time. Celebrities in town joined the festivities. James Caan stopped by. Vic Damone of Brooklyn, New York, came and stayed awhile.

"Jimmy Caan was doing a film in Chicago with Candy Bergen. It was his first time in the Mansion and he was fascinated by the scene. He was a nice kid. He and his brother were close. He envied me that kind of life, these chics all around. We got to be good friends."

The Harold Harris quintet played piano, sax, drums, bass. Chubby Checker sang and Twisted, and Bebop innovator Dizzy Gillespie was there.

"Man, got any grass, John?

"Yeah, I got grass."

"Shit, man—"and they lit up and talked and got smashed.

His star and that of Playboy's rose concurrently. Playboy clubs sprang up in Miami, St. Louis, Atlanta, Cincinnati, and Phoenix; and he traveled to them first class, broadening his horizon, embedding himself in an exciting, rootless way of life. Keith interviewed the women, and he interviewed the male personnel: room directors, general managers, bartenders. Keith trained Bunnies in stylized service: dignified behavior, lightheartedness, absolutely no physical contact in the club, properly fitting costume, Bunny ears geometrically fixed. Training periods lasted about two months in each city. A typical session began at one in the afternoon, and so a "scene" could run till the end of the night. Thus, nature would still grant him, as Casanova wrote, "the sweet requisite of sleep." He loved working with Keith.

"Keith Hefner was one of the nicest people I ever met. Like his brother, he was full of integrity. Once, I told him a lie I'd told a girl. We used to lie to girls like it was no big fucking deal. Keith was appalled that I would misrepresent myself. She'd asked me, 'Are you fooling around with somebody else?' 'Honest to God I'm not, I lied.' 'You should have told her what you were doing,' Keith tells me. 'But, Keith, I wanted to keep fucking her and still do my other thing.' He made me aware of the truth, which I used in a way that made sense to me."

Then, in the early 1970s, Keith Hefner left the company, and John was placed in charge of staffing all of the Playboy clubs with Bunnies. Power flowed through his Italian veins. His dark eyes sparkled with power, his smile beamed it. For he could take a beautiful, willing, relatively small-town woman and set her up as a Playboy Bunny in London or New

York or Jamaica, with a good salary and benefits, and from Bunny she could become a Haute Couture model or a movie star. The gorgeous women who applied were, for the most part, married, and many were bored. The glamorous world of Playboy was as appealing to these women as it had been to this Italian from Chicago's ghetto. That inner sparkle suppressed by the humdrum of married life ignited. All of a sudden you look good in a Bunny costume. Guys ogle at you. Stage-door Johnnies wait for you to get out of work in order to take you to breakfast.

"It fucked up their marriages. It fucked up their heads."

He was as human as the next guy, like his great forebear Dante, who, in Hell, retains his humanity so that he can feel the suffering shades' pain as well as his own, like fainting in a swoon after listening to Francesca da Rimini tell the tragic story of her illicit love affair. Power, human John Dante discovered, was a great aphrodisiac. He received direct propositions from women who would not have given John Aimola the American time of day. He took up those invitations from women "who knocked me out, I sure did." The Sultan of Sensuality; The Don of Sexuality—he sure did. He did not get attached, because the time for a conventional life had long passed. A few women grew attached to him and, though there was no circle of Hell reserved for heartbreakers, he went ahead and broke their hearts.

"I was a 40-year-old fucking around with 18-year-olds who were very impressionable."

In New York, women viewed the job of Playboy Bunny as a means to an end, thus skirting the realm of his power. They worked in theater, dance, "stuff like that. They were a little rougher about it. They understood everything. They had ambitions. They weren't looking to get laid"—which may have come as a gust of fresh, autumn New York air. He loved independent women.

"I loved Gloria Steinem. Under the name Marie Ochs, she took a job at the New York Playboy Club and wrote an exposé on the Bunnies. I was fascinated by her because she had the most perfect legs I'd ever seen in my life. She wore an orange Bunny costume and she was the only Bunny who wore glasses. She was given special dispensation. None of the girls could wear jewelry or glasses. They had to wear contacts. She was working in the gift shop. Her legs drove me up a tree they were so beautiful."

Here is how he got to live with Hugh Hefner and Shel Silverstein, and, at any one given time, 40 of the most beautiful women in the world.

Just as his new-found power was about to place thousands of beautiful, grateful, ambitious women in his indebtedness, Fate attempted a last-gasp effort to detour his path away from the Playboy life and into that of marriage, family, and home. John Dante got married, just as his great ancestor Dante Alighieri had married and had children before his exile from the city he loved, and then spent his remaining years traveling through the alternating cold and sweltering north on his faithful steed. Yes, once, for however brief a time--a tik-tik of his one weekend of bliss--there was a Mrs. John Dante. Finding that he survived his affair with Mrs.

Silva up in his office, and after Dante's Inferno burned down twice, his angel Renée with whom he did not trifle "because I respected her too much" brokered a deal whereby he bought 30% of a belly dance club called the Kismet. His passion for Gustav Doré's etchings of Dante's Inferno that had gone up in flames and the ingenious labor and his creativity that went into displaying them on his club's walls transferred to the Turkish theme of the Kismet. He spread kilim rugs on the floors and placed blue hookahs here and there. Slivers of blue smoke snaked through the air, which was permeated with the odors of molasses and incense. He hung stained-glass lamps all around like so many guys lynched by their own dicks. One exotic belly dancer, Sue Lewis, captured his imagination and derring-do. She was the second of the three mobsters' women he made love to. She was also hit man "Sheriff" Matolla's girlfriend.

"We fucked when he was out of town. If he had known I was messing with her, he would have killed me. When it came to women, there was no danger that could stop me."

A sense of invincibility, the excitement of loving a desirable woman amid tremendous danger carried over into the kind of power over women's lives that he was experiencing now. Enter the third and last of gangsters' women, the charming, stylish Blanche Gregory, who was Willie "Ice" Atorino's girlfriend. She was attractive all the more because of the conjoining of Ice's torture techniques and his sense of eroticism, his fellow "made" men saying of him that keeping his victims alive for hours with ice pick and blowtorch was tantamount to an erection lasting four hours. Blanche Gregory's comfort with such a man behind closed doors transferred to the elegant figure she cut in public. She would not leave the house without wearing hat and gloves, and perfectly coifed. But then—

"They broke up and vivacious, full of fun and stylish Blanche applied for a job in Playboy."

Enter the John Dante of Power. Had Ice Atorino called him, remembering his fencing operation in Cicero, all "tributes" paid in full? He got Blanche a job in Playboy, and they commenced an affair, while he and Keith Hefner trained her and other fledgling Bunnies and Bunny Mothers how to look good before going out on the floor, making sure the costume fit skintight and makeup applied just right. One auspicious night—

"John, where is our relationship going?"

"Going?" he repeated, incredulous. "My job is going around the country hiring girls, where can it go?"

"Well, we could get married. Nothing will change except that we'll hang our clothes in the same closet."

Tragically, she had fallen in love with him. If a tenth of the women with whom he had been intimate also loved him—that's about 1,600 women in love with one man. But he acquiesced. Maybe he could conjoin Husband, Homeowner and, God knows, Father, with the Playboy life. John doesn't say whether it was a civil marriage or whether they married in the eyes of God or whether he brought his new American wife, a Bunny Mother wearing gloves and hat, to his parents' walk-up flat on the west side. Right away, as he had warned her, he was off to Baltimore to staff and open the Playboy club there, then to London, where he spent a solid year opening the London Playboy club, interviews for the Bunny position spanning four days. In order to avoid Circle 3 of the Adulterers, he had to fend off the advances of 3,000 of the most sultry women in mesh stockings and high heels on the British Isles, all competing for 200 jobs that only he could grant. The job of Playboy Bunny came with good pay, health benefits, all expenses paid to Chicago, and an open invitation to all Mansion festivities. During his tenure of power (1969 to 1974), a Playmate of the Year received $100,000 in cash, plus a couple of hundred thousand in furs, and a car.

A British beauty in fitted mesh stockings and high heels is ushered into a well-heated dark room. She parades, strikes a pose. She cannot see John Dante sitting out in the darkness, but she can hear a clear, courteous, baritone voice intone, without the slightest trace of an accent:

"Well, Miss Jane, why do you want to become a Playboy Bunny?"

Not only must she possess physical beauty, but also personality and intelligence, like a Miss Universe contestant.

"O Mr. Dante—" breathless—"'*Sometime too hot the eye of heaven shines, And oft' is his gold complexion dimm'd; And every fair from fair sometime declines, By chance or nature's changing course untrimm'd: But thy eternal Summer shall not fade…'* Shakespeare sonnet number eighteen, Mr. Dante…'"

Meanwhile, across the Atlantic, Mrs. Dante rented "a gorgeous apartment on the north side and charged up the finest furniture at John Smyths. Blanche was extravagant. I was extravagant. It was a disaster."

The marriage was over, tossing him onto Hef's Mansion doorstep.

He and Hef had become "very friendly". They loved to play games. The clik-clik of billiard balls kissing and the rings and chimes of pinball pervaded the Mansion.

"I believe Hef always needed a best friend. I think he always needed somebody to do something with. Maybe he felt guilty about what he wanted to do and wanted to share that guilt. I was doing the things he liked, and I was enjoying it because I loved it."

Good game players provided competition, little else.

"Unlike celebrities, good players had to be on their best behavior. That is, not mess with Hef's ladies."

Hef designed icons for his favorite Monopoly players. John's was a pair of seamed stocking legs, his own a dude smoking a pipe, Bill Cosby's a cat smoking a cigar.

"Bill was doing gigs at the Playboy Hotels. He was very, very conscious about not creating any publicity that could get back to his wife. He was very much in love with her. He never smoked any dope. 'I'm high enough on life, all the time,' he said, and he was. Bill was one of my favorite people. He was just a funny dude. He found humor in everything. 'I'm gonna buy Ill-in-nois.' You'd try to bargain with him, and he says, raspy: 'No, I won't sell.' "

Then one fateful night while they were playing, he said to Hef:

"I'm getting a divorce and have to find an apartment."

Hef invited him to his office.

John Dante née Giovanni Aimola of Fossacesia, Italy walks through the Mansion's iron grille door, which shuts tight behind him. Before him looms the majestic marble foyer, and then he ascends three staircases and halts before a white door with one peephole and a brass plate that reads:

Si Non Oscillas, Non Tintinnare.
If You Don't Swing, Don't Ring.

Well, he certainly swings so he rings, and the great door opens for him. To his left, in the Red Room, lives Shel Silverstein, and to his right rises a glass partition. He knocks. Come in, he is told.

"Why don't you stay here until you find an apartment," Hef offers.

"It was like being invited into the Vatican, some holy place."

Gustav Doré, King Minos.
There dreadful Minos stands, gnashing his teeth.
***Dante's Inferno* V, 6.**

"Womp! Womp!" a thick powerful tail enwraps him, and he cannot move. He is fettered for life. Beyond life. Fallen, winged angels carrying prodding spikes keep him in place. Attempting to cover his naked shame, he looks up at the flat summit of a boulder. Crowned, bearded Minos, King of the Underworld, Guardian of Hell, reclines at his ease, toying with his tail. He has the body of Hercules, of a Chippendale dancer, of Harry Reems. He would be the envy of Michelangelo. He purveys his fresh fodder with eyes so terrible that they are seen solely by the poor tortured souls of his herd.

Hef assigned him a lovely three-and-a-half room apartment on the third floor, with a king-size bed, parlor, kitchenette, and bathroom. Deluxe room service 24/7. Dial 20 and order Brut and beluga, cheeseburgers and malted milks, anything he wanted.

"For me, Hef was a deity. I owed him my existence."

God could not have been more bountiful. Girls who were not working that particular night lounged around doing their nails, watching TV, swimming in the heated indoor pool.

"It was almost like a fraternity house or a sorority house."

From training director he was promoted to Assistant to Playboy Enterprises' President Hugh Hefner. He was placed in charge of hiring Mansion personnel, including a chef who made a delectable Beef Wellington that would warm the heart of porn star Linda Lovelace. Adding to his prestige was the role of maintaining and staffing Hef's new stretch DC-9 jet, with worldwide range. He'd become a sultan with both a fixed and a traveling harem, a sailor with women in 1,001 ports. His checkered yet interesting life had finally led him, inexorably, to Hugh Hefner, this complex, fascinating man. And his dream of always being in the proximity of beautiful women and making love to them had become reality. From his Bunny Hunts he brought the lucky women back home, two on each arm, smiling, whistling an Italian tune. He introduced them to his house mates.

"Ladies, say hello to Hef. Oh, and this is Shel Silverstein."

There was an ease, a nonchalance to living and loving in the Chicago Playboy Mansion. A contented Hef ducked in and out of fervent periods of work and play. Shel Silverstein became rich and famous and stayed a few months, then was off to Haight-Ashbury or Sausalito or Key West or New York City. The women who lived in the Mansion conducted their lives like it was their home. They dated and went out at their leisure, returning home in time for their tours at the clubs and photo shoots. Here comes the exclusive commercial subject matter Shel insisted that John write about because Shel witnessed it, saw with his own eyes, had become John Dante's confidante, and was the only man on earth to whom John showed his private Polaroids.

Often, before going out on a date, a Bunny or a Playmate would call and say,

"Okay to stop by, John?"

She'd given herself a few hours' leeway before her formal rendezvous later in the evening.

"We'd smoke a joint, maybe take a 'lude(quaalude), drop some LSD"—sharing a home-hearth trip before venturing out into the world—"I wasn't into coke much in the Chicago Mansion. Dressed up, smelling divine, in high heels, I'd fuck them or they'd give me a blowjob. Whatever. It was no big deal." He offers his sagacity on the subject of the stronger sex. Women are "—wily. They know what to give away and what not to give away. When to give it, when not to give it. Probably guys like me and celebrities got more out of women than their boyfriends because they had a mind to, a reason to. Then she could take you to Paradise."

He culled from his early years the great lessons of his life. After Susan Einway set him squarely on his lifelong path, in his local high school he was having sexual relations with Meg, and she told her best girlfriend, Cindy:

"It's so wonderful with Johnny. I can't describe how great he is!" Meg gives Cindy—a "good-looking W.A.S.P blonde"—Johnny's phone number, and she calls him.

"I'm throwing a party for Billy Mathews. You know Billy, my beau. Can you come over to help me plan it out?"

Sure. He knew even then, "She wanted me to fuck her," and he goes to her place and tells her--

"Why don't you fuck Billy Mathews? You like Billy. You fuck him, don't you?"

"No, I don't fuck Billy," she said. "And I'm not going to fuck him either, not now. I don't want him to think I'm that kind of girl."

But it was all right for Johnny Aimola to think that she was that kind of girl, because he had absolutely no future with her or any other W.A.S.P. blonde in the world.

He fucked Cindy, nonetheless, and kept fucking her while Billy Mathews courted her, and, at the same time, kept up his relations with Meg.

"I was screwing three girls in town."

Now he was screwing practically each and every one of the 40 women living under the Mansion roof. The women he brought home from his Bunny hunts who had a mind to he invited to his quarters for a "scene," as he called a sexual tryst. Sex was a Spectacular—John Dante Presents—a bacchanal of dizzying consciousness and exultant fornication that would have been the envy of the ancient Romans and Greeks. When he was about to have such a scene, he requested of the lady in question: "Would you dress in high heels and seamed stockings?" Invariably, she agreed. Before anything else, he requested further that his lover get on his bed and raise her seamed-stocking legs and part them--again, she complied. He had carried these fetishes with him as faithfully as he had carried his passion for Gustav Doré's etchings of *Dante's Inferno,* from the time of the feast days of his boyhood such as Christmas, Thanksgiving, and Easter, when his mother and her friends, including the Sicilian landlord known as "La Boss", made themselves up with circles of rouge on their full dark cheeks and dashes of bright red lipstick which streaked like fire across lips that had narrowed and curled from penury and disappointment, and on their knotty legs they donned sheer stockings with center seams that began at the narrow ankle top, split the muscular calf, and then rose up through the center of the inner thigh until the dark, straight embossed seam line disappeared beneath their pretty dresses and rose further, unseen, to the garter belt with clips.

Holding his Polaroid camera, he stood at the foot the bed, naked, with a hard-on, and snapped away.

"It was very erotic and stimulating fore-play [sic], and the ladies actually enjoyed doing it because it aroused me so much. We fucked, took more pictures, drank, fucked some more. Sex was a five-hour affair."

He was creating a visual archive in anticipation of the time when he wished to recall a particular lover and a particular scene. Over the course of his 40-year life in Playboy, he snapped 400 sets of Polaroid images, each set consisting of 40 to 50 pictures, each one-time snapshot consisting of a lover in seamed stockings and high heels. Five-hour sessions with around 16,000 lovers—that's at least 30,000 orgasms in private scenes alone, which vaulted him to the Sunday morning of his one weekend of ecstatic bliss.

Yes, this was the sort of material John Dante should write about. He and only he, save for one of its major progenitors, Hugh Hefner, was in a unique position in the history of America's sexual revolution of the 1960s and '70s to experience and tell of it. Further, no man other than John Dante in the 20th century could speak or write from first-hand experience on the nature of the Playboy Mansion Orgy. Get it straight from the horse's mouth.

Origin of the Playboy Mansion Orgy, According to John Dante

"Hef knew that I was screwing practically all of the girls and one night he says, nonchalantly, 'Why don't you guys come up and we'll watch a movie in my bedroom.' "

He and his lady of the evening may have been lounging around or snacking in the kitchen in their fresh white robes. Sure, why not, go up to Hef's spectacular bedroom and watch a film.

"I was pretty good at getting girls to come into the orgies, and Hef liked that. Probably he would have done the same himself, but he didn't bother. The girls worked shifts at the Playboy clubs. At two o'clock, a particular shift would come home, maybe 15 or 20 girls. At four o'clock, the last shift would come home. Sometimes we'd be upstairs playing games, Monopoly, and either Hef or I would say, 'Let's go to the Roman bath.' It was as simple as that. Some would come and some would not. Playmates would get involved, stay a few weeks and then leave. There was a constant flow of Playmates through the Mansion. They would stay at the Mansion while doing their shoots at the office."

A love feeling permeated their house. Lots of kissing and playing and romping amid the aromatic bubbles, everyone naked as the day they were born.

"Hef and I and 4 or 5 girls. It was ethereal. It was heavenly. The orgies were difficult for me in the sense that they ended at four, five in the morning, and I had to be at work at ten. It got to the point that I didn't show up at the office until two o'clock because I had to get some fucking sleep. After the orgies, Hef would go to sleep until the following night."

And then everything changed.

HOLLYWOOD, U.S.A.

"Go West Young Man," 19th-century journalist Horace Greeley's advice to the venturesome alluded to the discovery of gold in Sutter's Mill in Colonia, California, during the 1850s, not an ingot of which John Aimola sifted 100 years later. But his enterprising, restless friend Hef decided to go west for reasons of a different sort, yet equally golden—Hollywood, U.S.A. Toward the middle of the 1970s, Hef purchased a second Playboy mansion in Los Angeles, California.

"Hef was totally burnt out from a company that had expanded out of his control"—monthly magazine sales in the millions, growing number of Playboy clubs, resorts, hotels and casinos—"and he had always been fascinated by movie stars. He was a big celebrity freak. Screen stars, celebrities, could do no wrong in his house."

In Los Angeles, Hef would be surrounded by beauty and glamour, and established and emerging movie stars would have easy access to his house, an opulent refuge from paparazzi, yellow journalists, and frenzied fans. In the transition stage, the Playboy jet which John managed facilitated movement between Chicago and Los Angeles. He staffed the flight to Los Angeles with 15 Bunnies from the Chicago Playboy clubs and the flight to Chicago with 15 Bunnies from the Los Angeles club. They returned to Chicago and Los Angeles via regularly scheduled flights. As for his hiring practices—

"Sometimes I gravitated to my personal tastes. Good-looking legs, great figure, tits, face. Hair and skin didn't matter. In fact, Ginger Miles was one of my honeys. We fooled around with the Jet Bunnies, especially on the trip to Africa."

It was a million-dollar memory flying 30,000 feet in the air with Ginger Miles in his arms, the black night sky studded with the stars and the moon just outside their window.

In time, Hef decided to move kit and caboodle to Los Angeles. His Playboy Enterprises was like an ambulant revolutionary government with its own constitution and officers which, under siege, moved up to the mountains.

"John didn't move to Los Angeles right away," states Frank D'Rone.

The City of Angels was two thousand miles away from his adopted home ground of Chicago, the old neighborhood, his aging parents, the Chicago gangsters, and Luigi, Frank, Tony, and Petey. On the other hand, though Hef was a mobile deity, there was only one Vatican, Hef's Mansion, which had become "a womb to me." The Mansion had become like the womb of his courageous mother—warm, nutritious, delicious. He grew in this sacred house called the Playboy Mansion the way he had grown unwanted, except by his mother, inside of her. Imagine a fetus on leave from the womb a few hours at a time--that's how he felt when he took Looie for a walk or to the vet's or drove over to the west side or out to the airport and the Playboy jet. Of course, he would take Looie with him to Los Angeles along with his Polaroid camera and his hundreds of transfer cases filled with Polaroid stills so that from time to time he could take a look and remember a given Chicago lover on a given Chicago night. The climate out there was closer to Acapulco and Fossacesia, and it could get real hot. Maybe he could find an L.A. equivalent to Dante's Inferno. Yes, the L.A. Mansion could suit Gentleman John Dante. It snuggled in the Holmby Hills so it was more rural, spread out over five acres, a peaceful, retiring, bucolic setting in which a gentleman of vast experience and worth could write his memoirs. He would not have to leave the grounds. There was a grotto like the one on Capri, a fountain like Rome's Trevi, and an aviary from which chirruping, prancing sparrows and blue jays would herald the end of the night and an orgy. A pet cemetery, assuring, if it came to that, a first-class send-off for the poodles. Guest rooms numbered in the dozens for the friends he had made in Chicago who went on to become stars based in Hollywood, like Don Adams, Jimmy Caan, and Tony Curtis. Shel Silverstein would move his quarters out there. There was a Bath House for special scenes, and Mansion Nights—Fight Night, Movie Night—would carry over. Night was night, long and sizzling, filled in all climates with beauty and love, beneath the orbs of the firmament. Game Night would have its own house, as the previous owner was a chess aficionado who wanted the great game of war's most powerful piece, the queen, to have her own arena. Mansion West had ivy on the walls like on the walls of Ivy League schools, where Italians of his generation were not entirely welcome. Finally, there was a wishing well so every day he would toss a coin down there and wish to live out his waning years in the land of his birth, in Florence, the Renaissance city of his great forebear Dante.

The problem was, how could be useful out there? Sommelier for the wine cellar? Hef's *consigliere,* principal advisor on all matters amorous and otherwise? For, at this time, he suffered a great change in his life, too-

-he quit his job at Playboy. He gave up his large salary with benefits and power's aphrodisiac that came with hiring Bunnies and Bunny Mothers and the prestige of maintaining and staffing the Playboy jet, embracing Meg Miles through the clouds.

"I left for personal reasons which I will go into in the book."

But he did not get around to it, as Death is a walk-in, needing no appointment.

Shel must have known that John had quit his job in Playboy midway through their life together as Playboy cronies, for Shel lived with John and was the housemate John confided in, sharing their moods, ups and downs. Hef certainly knew, but John does not include such conversation and event in his notes. From his notes and tapes, one can say that his friendship of 40 years with Hef played out like a kind of silent film wherein the actors themselves do not mouth words to one another, yet there seemed so little time to get to know this beautiful woman or that one. John ascribes so few quotes to Hef. "We're having a thing tonight." "Don't worry about it." At the heart of the Great Lover John Dante's life was another man. Perhaps Hef loved John for his quality of having been sorely injured a long time before but would never speak of it, complain about it, pity himself for it. It was simply a deep wound which he carried with dignity.

Noel Cunningham, master chef and close friend of John's during the 1980s who grew to love him, offers a reason why John quit his job at Playboy.

"John felt that a lot of people around Hef were blood-suckers, hangers-on, those with stock options and bloated expense accounts. They drove John crazy. John was the only one who told Hef straight up."

The scale of the true fiber of his life had tipped toward friendship over career. He refused to be part of the exploitation of his great friend Hef. Dante's Inferno had burned down twice as a result of his integrity, he quit his job as a result of it—what would happen in Los Angeles?

"I was still Hef's friend and he wanted me to move to Los Angeles with him."

"Ach—what the hell? He would give it a try. Keep one foot in Chicago and one in Los Angeles, just as Hef had done.

John Dante, private collection

"In Los Angeles I had to compete with movie stars, producers, and agents for the affection of the prime ladies."

With the thousands of women with whom John Dante was intimate, in private scenes and in orgies, his overwhelming desire was always to arouse a woman's affection for him.

In the Playboy Mansion West, Sunday Night was Movie Night, and he comes up and sits at one end of the front-row couch and Hef sits in the other.

"No one sat on the couch unless Hef invited you."

Chloe comes out and sits next to him.

"Wow! I'm going to be fucking around with Chloe--" Hef, the 20th-century's Architect of Sex, had arranged the coupling beforehand—"I was pleased because I had seen Chloe's porno flicks, she was a hot little number."

Then Sheryl comes out and sits next to Hef. The post-film orgy roster was set: Hef-Sheryl/John-Chloe.

The lights go out and the film begins to roll. He doesn't recall the film—*Reds? Bonnie and Clyde?* because about two minutes in--here comes John Reed and Clyde Barrow rolled into one.

"Warren ducks under the lights so as not to disturb the images on the screen and sits between Chloe and Sheryl. Hef had arranged a scene between him and Warren and the two girls. I rationalize—Jesus Christ, if I were a girl, who would I want to be fucking? This handsome mega-movie star or…or…" How was Hef or anyone else, including himself, supposed to introduce him in Los Angeles. "Uh, this is John Dante, former nightclub owner back in Chicago. Carved flames on Dante Inferno's roof with a chainsaw. Used to go out on Bunny Hunts. So give him a swing."

"It would be tantamount to me wanting to screw Lana Turner or Betty Grable."

Monday Night was Fight Night, and Jack Nicholson comes to watch the fights. He had already gained worldwide fame for *Easy Rider* and *Five Easy Pieces* and, at the time of this Fight Night, was Randolph McMurphy in *One Flew Over the Cuckoo Nest.* One inferno into another. Mr. Nicholson had a girlfriend in the world of Playboy, exactly in what capacity John does not say, and she was *his* girlfriend, too. He had managed to rouse the affection of one prime lady under the sun of Los

Angeles. This particular lady liked him for himself, sans persona of a Dante or suave former gangster or Playboy higher-up. She was willing to take him to Paradise because he was a good man, generous and nice, recognizing in him those personal characteristics that endeared him to Hef, Shel, Noel, Don, Frank, Luigi, Petey. This discerning prime lady became his Thursday girl. All of a sudden—

"I gave her three or four more days because we had such fun together."

With two simultaneous lovers, she was a woman of great breadth, but then reality reared its ugly head.

"Whenever Jack called her, he would get first choice, and it annoyed the shit out of me until I said to myself: 'Are you a shmuck? Is your ego that bad that you could get pissed off because this woman would rather see this mega movie star over you, and he was the guy who she was going out with first and you're the one who's the intruder?' "

A Great Lover such as John Dante has a wise inner voice. A Great Lover such as John Dante knows when to subsume his ego to the pleasure of his lover. A Great Lover's affairs do not age. He does not say whether this generous lover of two great men continued on as such for any length of time. Perhaps "What happened?" went by the wayside along with the conventional life. I inquired in his hellhole in Fort Lauderdale whether he kept in touch with any of his lovers from his Playboy days, and he answered yes, one had come down with cancer and another had gone on to a film career. He did not provide names, for they had names of a different sort:

I WAS A PRIME LADY WHO LOVED JOHN DANTE.

Nor could he compete for a prime lady's affection over the rock stars who visited their house in Los Angeles. That other evening around eight when he went up to hang out or eat—

"Hef was sitting on the divan with Mick Jagger, a bunch of girls around them and, nearby, Keith Richards is sitting on a chair, five or six girls around him. Mick—stoned out of his fucking gourd, almost on the floor, not even talking, and the women waiting for him to do anything, belch, fart. They were mesmerized by the Rolling Stones. They could have taken any one of the girls by the hand and walked upstairs without a word. Rock stars were the big celebrities for the girls between 18 and 30. Keith sitting there, scraggle-toothed, ugly, drawn, the girls grouped around him, waiting for him to do something, say something."

He did an about-face and went back down to his room.

PIG NIGHT

The next night, a Thursday, he looked in his mirror—he was a pig! His feet had four toes each, and he lifted one into the sink, wet it, and brought it up to his face to clear off the mud. His skin color was still dark—he had become an Italian pig. His snout was a long, hard, thick bone. His small eyes looked down at his outward curving tusk and then behind himself—he had a corkscrew tail. He tried to say something. "Unn-un," he grunted. Again: "Eeww," he squealed. His hearing was more acute. Filtering through his window were other squeals and grunts, like a corral of feeding pigs making siren sounds similar to a whale's. He hoofed over to the window. Celebs and guys he had never seen before were fucking pink, juicy, sweet sows all over the grounds. The cacophony of languorous squeals and staccato grunts were those of the sows' orgasms, for a sow's clitoris is large and thick, consisting of two nail-like structures at the tip.

"Thursday night was Pig Night, when the lesser guys on the Mansion list were expected to bring women who were not scrutinized for their looks but were expected to be "7's" or "8's". Hundreds of women came in the hope of becoming Playmates or getting onto the permanent guest list. The Playmates called it 'Pig Night.' They could not be seen. They wouldn't have anything to do with the common bimbos."

Once again, John Dante was nowhere to be found. He was not down in his room in the L.A. mansion and he was not in his quarters in the Chicago mansion. It was around Thanksgiving 1974—maybe he was home with his family, and the women including landlord La Boss had grown stouter but still bright and glowing in lipstick and rouge and powerful legs with seamed stockings and high heels placing with pride the fat, juicy turkey on the decorative table. How Hef missed him in Chicago and in Los Angeles and wants him out where the sun sings. Just look at Hef's Thanksgiving photo with note, he and his special lady of the time smiling out at him—and there's Shel home for the holiday, and Hef's loyal secretary Bobbie Arnstein, a sorrowful remnant of her once beautiful self, trying a smile. Everyone looking happy on this great American holiday, but Hef's expression is dead serious, he is saying something beyond language, something from the heart, an invitation to come in and see and hear his love.

Don't be a coward. Go back and give it another try. Because in Hell, the Cowards, those who had lived up in the clear light without praise and without infamy, run in circles and attract wasps and flies, which, in turn—

"streaked their faces with their blood, which, mingled with their tears, fell at their feet, where it was gathered up by sickening worms."
--Dante's Inferno, Canto 3, 69.

A 'fence,' he had been a fence, buying and selling stolen goods—certainly, that is not sitting on the proverbial fence. Nor is an Italian from the ghetto who goes on to build from scratch a classy nightclub where the people of Chicago had gone and relaxed and out of the corner of their eyes glimpsed scenes from Hell. A Coward would not have dared to fondle his substitute grammar school teacher's breasts. Or fuck three gangsters' women without trepidation.

A long, sleek black limousine pulls up to the Mansion's security guard's station. The passenger side window lowers, and the guards looks in at the driver in a black suit and white gloves, artificial night light glinting off his back vinyl cap, who directs the guard's eyes to the back seat and a shade of a man in dark glasses, a black poodle on his lap. A second white limousine pulls up behind the entering Town Car with a large dog's head jutting out from the passenger side window, taking in the refreshing night breeze, tongue out and wagging—that of the canine Rufus, a mix of bloodhound and "some other big dog [a two-year-old Great Dane with sandy hair]." The entire car belongs to Rufus, for he is a dog's dog, a great lover among dogs. In the pantheon of dogs along with

Lassie, Toto, and Rin-Tin-Tin. Tomorrow night, Royal Rufus will be the co-star in a real-life sex scene with porn star Linda "Deep Throat" Lovelace in the Mansion Bath House. The gamekeeper leashes Rufus and walks him to the kennel.

He may have stayed away because of a prime blood-sucker, hanger on, bottom feeder, as he liked to say, a man so odious that, in Hell, his name:

"I am Hard Boots. I was the one who knocked Linda Lovelace down then kicked her with my hard boots."

Hard Boots was Linda Lovelace's, née Linda Boreman, manager, who watched her trysts through whatever holes he could find or make, like in paintings on the walls, certainly keyholes, and time and again held a Webley 8-shot automatic to her temple while threatening to kill her sister and her sister's children. The name "Lovelace" was given to her by the director of the porn classic *Deep Throat*, about a woman whose clitoris is in her throat in an inordinately wide esophagus, like a sword swallower able to take down a 3-foot sword. Her black-and-blue marks powdered over for the opening swimming pool scene in *Deep Throat*—how could anyone, Hef included, know that they were the result of a terrible beating Hard Boots administered to Linda Boreman the night before in their motel room, punching her down to the moldy carpet, and then kicking her with his boots, whereupon she folded in the fetal position and tried to fend off kicks to the head and breasts and stomach with her arms and hands. For Linda Boreman, Hard Boots was highly believable. His latest command—

"Tomorrow, you will fuck Rufus in the Bath House."

Linda Lovelace's scene with another dog back east—Harmon, a tall, skinny, tan dog, while Hard Boots watched from behind the camera, was popular among 8-mm XXX-film collectors, headed at the time by a Far Eastern gentleman with centuries more of pornography in his culture. Attempts at staging scenes between women and dogs often failed, the dogs freezing and backing off, because the women moved. Women in such a position had to be like Dante's menacing She-Wolf found in Canto 1, where Dante, lost in a wood in the middle of his life, as John Dante is now, comes upon a She-Wolf with yellow, peering eyes who guards the mountain that leads to Paradise and his muse and love, Beatrice. This She-Wolf, inherently powerful, appears to be still but is moving closer and closer, imperceptibly. The woman in a scene with a dog must contain all the attraction that a dog desires, without moving. An immobile Linda Lovelace had fucked Harmon for two solid hours and so, if she could do it on the East Coast, she could do it on the West Coast, and, if she could do it on film, she could do it in the flesh.

The night before, a scene was held in the Jacuzzi, kind of like a wedding weekend of multifarious festive activities. Hard Boots was out to show how pleased Linda Lovelace was with the prospect of fucking Rufus. Someone held her from underneath so that she was propped up on the warm, swirling water's surface, then someone else fist-fucked her. A female participant stepped in and she fist-fucked Linda Lovelace, too. The Porn Queen was ready. Rufus was fully rested. The rest of the night filled with stars and the moon passed tranquilly, and the next morning a roiling sun rose over Los Angeles.

Hard Boots and Linda Lovelace and a "select few, of which I was one of the privileged" march over to the Bath House. A guard stands at the door, for this night would be a propitious one for a police raid. The kennel keeper hands the leashed Rufus to a second guard, who promptly walks Rufus to the Bath House. This guard joins the guard at the door. Hard Boots commands Linda Lovelace:

"Take off your clothes."

She undresses and goes down onto all fours "on the carpeted section of the floor," and then waits, unmoving. All *ochos humanus* glue to the duo. Did such onlookers derive interest from imagining his/herself the half-horse/half-human centaurs of Circle 7 Bolgia 1, who gallop around the Murderers in Hell's River of Blood, shooting arrows into them so that they stay down. Or the half-bull/half-man Minotaur which lords over the whole of Circle 7, which, in addition to the Murderers, includes the Suicides and the Sodomites. The poet Dante is non-committal about whether Minotaur's head or torso is that of a bull. Both Dantes left food for the imagination.

Though Linda Lovelace is absolutely still, Rufus backs off. Hard Boots fights for time. No one was in any special hurry.

When Linda Lovelace was down in Florida with Hard Boots, she managed to steal a few moments to inquire of a prostitute with experience with dogs how to go about it. She wanted to know what went into a successful scene so that she could sabotage it. First, the prostitute advised, get naked. A dog's form of foreplay is placing his paws on your shoulder. Do not look him in the eyes and, most importantly, do not move. The dog will lick and kiss you energetically. Be ultra-passive. Touching the dog anywhere will frighten it. Once you notice that the dog has picked up your scent, go down onto all fours. Stay in one spot and wait for the animal to come to you. Once the dog begins to fuck you, still do not move. Each and every time the dog withdraws his cock—breathe.

Back in the Mansion Bath House, Linda Lovelace stands erect on her knees, and Rufus comes and places his paws on her shoulders, and then, picking up her scent, licks and licks. She goes down and is perfectly still. Rufus approaches. He rises up behind her—but then drops down to all fours. The large dog pauses, looking baffled, as is everyone who is watching. Again, Rufus backs away.

"Nothing happened," Linda Lovelace writes in her memoir, *Ordeal.*

Maybe she had made a subtle internal movement that could not be seen by the naked human eye, one that produced an internal smell that only a dog in Rufus' position could pick up, that very smell produced by Dante's She-Wolf of Canto 1 who frightened the pilgrim and caused him to shriek as much from a smell emanating from her as her appearance, a smell first subtle then overwhelming, that of excrement, produced by an unseen, slight yet powerful internal movement, the alternate contraction and tightening of the sphincter.

The night sky above Los Angeles is black and clear, studded with shimmering stars and smiling moon. The orbs of the firmament have cleared away the day's detritus. The lights are on in the Game House, and the sounds of Pinball—chimes, bells, buzzers, flippers flapping—filter out into the warm night air. Inside, Hef is intent on a game. A clock with a large face on the wall reads 11:20. The night is young. A shade wearing an inestimable smile sidles up beside Hef and places a hand against the wall and watches the bright, raucous world of the Pinball playfield under the glass. In all its time away, through all the blacks and whites, the shade had not for a single moment lost interest in a game.

"And now it is after midnight. Hefner is in the Game House of his mansion. Of all the women who have passed through his homes during these 25 years, it is not a woman to whom Hefner has been loyal. The person who has lived with him the longest is a man, a man named John Dante. Dante is Hefner's best friend; they met in Chicago and Dante has lived with Hefner for 13 years. Tonight Hefner and Dante play pinball. Six past and future Playmates, uniformly gorgeous, sit on a couch and watch the endless games."

--Bob Greene, *The Free Lance Star.*

Courtesy John Dante, private collection

3: ORGY

"The private parties up in Hef's bedroom were mind-boggling. Women with hardly any experience with sex found themselves in situations that were impossible for them to imagine."--John Dante

"In Los Angeles, Hef became the playboy he had always wanted to be. He fully realized the power he had over young women. They came in droves. The ratio of women to men was 10 to 1."

The way a Sultan's mother had the sole key to her son's harem's bedrooms, according to John Dante, Sultan Hef was the only one who laid down inviolable rules governing his house. Be young and beautiful and leave all inhibitions at the front gate. No boyfriends and husbands allowed. Men are allowed through the front gate only if they bring women who meet with Hef's approval. Hef and a few celebrities and insiders have free rein in the Mansion because Hef well understands how hard men and women have to work to achieve august stature.

By providing a safe, private, elegant refuge for established and emerging film stars, Hugh Hefner is, perhaps, the greatest film preservationist/restorative agent of the mid-20th, early-21st centuries.

The superior supply of beautiful, generous women in Los Angeles produced subtle changes in the nature of the Mansion orgy. Whereas in Chicago there had been "a love feeling, almost like a fraternity or sorority," here—

"The private parties up in Hef's bedroom were mind-boggling. Women with hardly any experience with sex found themselves in situations that were impossible for them to imagine."

No matter what eyewitness John Dante could possibly say or write about these orgies, or however skillfully a writer could help him craft them, they remain beyond the pale of human imagination.

Novice orgy participants familiar with their boyfriends' and husbands' wants and desires who had sat in dark movie theaters ogling their favorite movie stars—could it possibly be that here they come in the flesh and blood, wearing fresh white robes, walking into the self-same bedroom, all smiles, already having a rollicking good time, not only in the warm willing flesh, but also the rare mind set of no yesterdays, no tomorrows, no prevailing sense of ownership. The movie stars exist in the imagination and only for the duration of this particular orgy—outside of real time and adequate power of human memory. This was real life where famous movie stars treated you like a romantic interest, with the sole object of honest-to-goodness hours of fun and foreplay and fornication. Arriving at the mountaintop, all orifices gorged—turn and watch yourself having sex while you are having it, or rewind so as to feel this way over and over again, forever young in the arms of your favorite movie stars, making love to them, having them make love to you, your ear on their rapidly beating, exultant hearts.

THREE ORGIES

As if by his great friend Shel Silverstein's urging, John Dante goes on to describe three Mansion orgies in some detail. Shel's brows raise, his eyes twinkle with satisfaction. This is what will sell. This is what will get you to Florence and then some. At the same time, John Dante's triumvirate of orgies comprise the whys and wherefores of his hellish shrieks.

He begins his descent with a bit of Mansion orgy protocol.

"Hef would send Haley to my quarters."

How many times had Hef dispatched Haley down to his quarters and then the orgy progressed with satisfaction to all three? Does one ever tire of viewing Leonardo's "Portrait of a Young Girl" or Michelangelo's "Pietà"? Hef/Haley/John—each knew what to expect, for routine existed in the Mansion as in well-run affairs and households. Hef dispatching Haley down to John's room a number of times was an act of enduring friendship on Hef's part. He knew full well which of the prime ladies in their house John liked, as he said, "to cock around with." By this time, the mid-to-late 1970s, they had been best of friends for 15 years and had lived together longer than with the women of their conventional marriages and any of the hundreds of Bunnies and Playmates who dropped in like beautiful swallows, stayed long enough to work and to love, then flew away. But now, in this particular "thing," something different, something cataclysmic, was about to happen.

With long blonde hair radiant as a blazing sun, golden curls falling around her square shoulders, skin taut, smooth and firm, efflorescent perfume filling the staircase, Haley descends happily to John's room. She knocks resolutely on his door. He is showered, mildly perfumed, and wears his freshened white robe. One advantage of being a permanent Mansion resident was that you possessed your own Orgy robe. Guests invited into a scene were supplied with robes, which, afterward, were left behind. John's robe, though still pure white and soft as heather, retained his handsome imprint and the appealing natural odor of his corporeal self. He opens his door—there's Haley, beaming, her robe drawn, and, while his eyes look down to her high heels, with a flourish and a smile he ushers her in. Standing before him in the flesh and blood is the realization of always being in the proximity of a prime lady, with the prospect of making love to her. Haley, smiling deeply into his eyes, flashes open her robe and, at the same time, whirls around and models for him. She has decorated her long, shapely legs with seamed stockings and anchored them with high heels, knowing full well that John Dante was, is, and always will be the Czar of Seamed Stockings and High Heels. Arms around waists, they ascend to Hef's bedroom. Along the way, there are no hushed voices, and no shadows flit on back stairwells. Their house was not a secretive, furtive one. Hef's bedroom door is open and there he is, waiting.

"Hef spent maybe a million and a half, two million to do his bedroom. All carved wood, statues of women, fantastic sound system, two 6'x 6' TV screens so that you could watch yourself having sex as you're having it, and it was also recorded. The fucking bed was almost the size of my place now. And the carpet—light beige. Headboard with remote controls for rewinding, music and sex toys."

A bacchanal fit for the Caesars would not be complete without a Roman bath, so Hef built one beneath his fantastic bedroom, a short ride down, made of Italian marble, loaded with bubbles and echoing music, which could accommodate 18 or 19.

Haley and John start off by having sex on Hef's fantastic bed.

"She was sucking me and Hef was watching--" was it really Hef? because "we were stoned, drugged out with grass and coke and poppers and all that jazz." Lying back, Haley sucking him, his fig bolstered by images of seamed stockings and high heels on the screen of his mind—"fig," that's what the hooded Benedictine monks called genitals, stemming from Sandro Botticelli's eternal painting "The Birth of Venus," the Goddess of Love curvaceously naked, her fiery, serpentine hair cascading down and across her flaming pubis, concealing it. While Haley's warm breath and thick red lips and slithering tongue played with his protended fig, Hef watched, stimulated, relaxed. In the way that, in his private scenes, John's foreplay was snapping Polaroids of his lovers, watching, at least in this scene, seemed to be a form of Hef's foreplay. Watching, a visual/aural aphrodisiac. Watching a man he loved deriving pleasure from a woman he also loved and desired. Watching their faces and bodies inflame with lust. Relegating human reason to secondary stature. Watching naked, aroused bodies hungering for one another and all the myriad forms that that takes. Watching a procession of free, happy men and women in his house in the flesh and blood, and, at the same time, on screen.

Sex for Hef and John was like dinner for Italians, a culture, and the American pastime of baseball. Multifarious foreplay to dinner takes the form of traffic on the streets diminishing, the rush-hour throng of pedestrians thinning, start-up of the symphony of pots and pans filtering out to the streets, bars displaying chips and nuts and aperitifs to whet the appetite. Dinner itself unfolds over hours, late into the night, concluding with brandies and biscotti, figs and nuts, and then the leisure way home, and, finally, love, a kiss before sleep. In a Playboy orgy, as in baseball, there was no set time, ending upon the home team's final turn at bat. A Playboy scene of sex, according to John Dante, ended at the end of the night, when the birds in the aviary began to chirrup, heralding the new day's sun. About sustaining the bliss of their orgies, his and Hef's:

"We learned how to control it. We had laid three or four times the same women privately in out apartments. It was almost like a marital thing."

Laying the same women a couple of times whether in the privacy of his apartment or the public of his best friend amounted to John Dante's notion of marriage. Whether their communal sex unfolded up in Hef's bedroom or down in the Roman bath or in the warm, swirling waters of the Jacuzzi or somewhere on the grounds—"There was fucking going on all over the place"—either he or Hef would turn to the other and say:

"Don't come yet. We've got a lot of time here."

Up in Hef's bedroom, it seemed that he was lying back with Haley down around him for an eternity, but then he felt a playing around his mouth.

"I looked—Haley was kissing me! I was being kissed and I was still being sucked, and it was Haley who was kissing me. Suddenly, I felt something rise in me. I was getting flaccid..."

Sssss—it has begun to rain in John Dante's heart and on the Gluttons of Circle 3. Rain gray with filth intermingled with hailstones and snow which fall onto Hell's ground, which is the texture and stench of human shit. An incessant, cold, heavy rain which streaks across Hell's shadowed air, tearing into the suffering shades, ripping their skin, and they howl like dogs. There it is—Cerberus! the demon dog with three eyes and three heads and three gullets and three filthy snouts. It does not matter what type of individual human the tortured shade was up in the light nor its memories or dreams. Down here, the shade is reduced to the ungranted wish that it be struck blind so as not to see the great worm's brimming mouths. Like the Glutton Ciacco of disordered appetites—excessive eating, drinking, fucking—his bare skin ripped to shreds by the razor-sharp rain, his remaining paltry shreds torn further by Cerberus' hooked talons, unrecognizable to the pilgrim who knew him up in the clear light. Ciacco looks pleadingly at Dante for one instance of solace, one moment of recognition for the good deeds he had performed. But his eyes begin to turn, imperceptibly, and then his head bows, and then the rest of him collapses into the filthy gutter, like a drunkard.

His great fear that his steed might stumble or refuse to begin another race was assuaged by the pleasure his love making invoked. Looking up at a lady of a private scene smiling as he rolled down her seamed stockings. Gazing upon her in ecstasy with one eye, with the other eye fixed on the same ecstasy over at their images on the TV. Naked, hard, focusing his Polaroid camera down to her dressed and posing for him with pleasure on his bed because she knew how much he liked this foreplay. Each and every one of his thousands of lovers possessed a special language of the moment of their ecstasy—and, perhaps, to Shel Silverstein's satisfaction, one or more may have told him what they felt. But now he fought against freeing himself from Haley's deepening kiss, against turning his face a few degrees to see what was showing on the TV screens—most of all, employing all of his strength and all of his history against looking down and seeing a man, any man, with his limp cock in that man's mouth. Because if he looked and it was, indeed, a man, especially his best friend Hef, and his eyes locked on, say, Hef's quizzical, beseeching, dispirited eyes, those eyes would begin to turn, imperceptibly, and then his head would bow, and they would not exchange another friendly glance for all eternity, and then the rest of him would collapse into the filthy gutter, like a drunkard.

"I let him do it to me three or four times because I enjoyed fucking around with Haley. She was the one I enjoyed most at that time—

my W.A.S.P. fantasy, beautiful, beautiful blonde girl. And I didn't want to upset the status quo. I was afraid of leaving the Mansion."

The Mansion was his only real home. His father Aimola had waited for him and his mother and their battered suitcase at Chicago's Union Station because he did not have the money to meet them in New York, then they took a bus to a walk-up in Little Italy. Then there was his room in the Welcome Inn in Wisconsin's back woods, then another room which doubled as his office at Dante's Inferno, where he took the gangster's woman and the whole front staircase burned down. Something else that Shel Silverstein may have known—John did not know how to live anywhere else.

Had he let whoever the fuck was down there do it to him four or five times during the same ménage à trois, relenting to his persistent desire to replace Haley after he, John, had beseeched her—"Please, baby, please…" and she went back down and replaced the man and renewed bestowing upon him "the greatest gift a woman can give to a man," then the undesired man moved aside and watched awhile before succumbing once again to overwhelming desire. Or had there been four or five separate scenes with myriad other participants but always with Haley and Hef? The repetition over time of simultaneous Paradise and Hell etched in his mind, and he carried the conjunction in the silver Isuzu with the tandem Looie and Dino poking out the passenger side window, taking the breeze.

Four or five times Haley floats down to his quarters, her long blonde hair radiant as the sun, her peignoir billowing, exposing the chiaroscuro of black line of seamed stockings running from her narrow, sharp ankles up her fair, firm inner thighs, smiling, her ivory teeth sparkling. She knocks at his door, beckoning, and he opens it and meets her smile with one of his own and then ushers her in, and she whirls around and models his fetishes. Together, they are the essence of chiaroscuro. Her fair American skin against his dark Italian. She the glory of the sun, he the epitome of shadow. Along with their seamed stockings and high heels and valiant souls, the Italian women of his old neighborhood had mustaches and sideburns, and little hairs sprouted from their resolute chins. Blonde W.A.S.P.s were customarily out of reach. Hef himself was W.A.S.P. All that Giovanni Aimola, a.k.a. John Dante, was not. FUCK ALL THAT YOU ARE NOT.

Never for a moment had he considered that Hef dispatched Haley down to him because she asked him to, that it was she who requested this ménage à trois, and, knowing exactly who he was and what he liked, she went down to bestow it upon him. What better proof of this one woman called Haley's love for him than, longing to merge fellatio with a kiss, she rose up, hovered close to his ecstatic face with closed eyes, lowered her full, moist, warm lips to his—and kissed him. Had he not felt the yearning of her soul through her lips? So profound had been her desire for him that there may not have been another man down there at all, just the resonance, the echo of her greatest gift. What better proof of her love when "Please, baby, please--"and she goes back down and merges with her echo and proceeds to take him home. And then four or five times, Haley ascends with him to Hef's million-dollar bedroom where his great friend awaits on his bed, and he lies back, stoned, and envisions Haley naked beneath her lingerie, save for the tracking of her stockings' black seams. Unbeknownst to him, her knees bend and crease, while her fair, bony hands brace on the giant mattress and her slight weight shifts imperceptibly to the balls of her feet, her heels lifting off the beige carpet. Her salacious mouth opens and, forthwith, he feels his hard fig slide through her pressing red lips and into her warm, viscous mouth. But then he feels a feint, unexpected tickling around his mouth. He opens his glazed eyes—Haley is kissing him! Wait a second, she is supposed…

The nebulous "something" surfacing inside of him, and going flaccid in the man's mouth—now that "something" takes on form, a pen-and-ink outline of a featureless face, composed of solid black bars streaking in helter-skelter fashion. "Something" unfinished yet powerful, as powerful as the She-Wolf of incontinence with red-ringed eyes inching closer, and closer, imperceptibly. As powerful as Michelangelo's Bound Slaves found in the Galleria dell'Accademia in Florence, which he will visit one day. The great artist left these sculptures, which line the corridor that tourists pass on their way in to view the original David, unfinished, believing that the singular torsos chiseled and chipped, smoothed and refined out of rough slabs of Carrara marble were of such explosive power at rest that it rendered the rest—head, limbs, mind, memory, loins—unnecessary. Their inherent powerful incompletion was their completion. John Dante would have been content living out his incomplete life the way it was, where it was. The papacy forbade access to cadavers for the purpose of studying human anatomy so, in the dead of night, flitting like shadows, his great ancestors Michelangelo and Leonardo da Vinci disinterred corpses from gravesites. If only they could have come to the Playboy Mansion and, holding pad and charcoal, sat on the lip of the swimming pool or on the rim of the Jacuzzi and looked and meditated on the exquisite physical forms of the Chippendale Dancers,

Harry Reems, Tony Curtis, Warren Beatty, James Caan, John Dante, and Hugh Hefner. A photo of the David beside the photo of John Dante in the Mansion swimming pool holding, instead of a slingshot, his beloved poodle Looie—David's and John's torsos are smooth, of well-defined musculature, and exude relaxed power.

That powerful "something" that arose in him finally opens out to a blazing hot day from the time of his boyhood on Chicago's west side, at the beginning of World War II, his homeland of Italy in the process of mechanizing its military. He loved to make lead soldiers and play inside with his best friend Dominick and, when the sun finally came out, go down the block out of view of the great Italian immigrant women watching to the lead foundry, where they made soldier kits and lead molds used in making the bullets for the revolvers and rifles and machine guns that would go into killing six million soldiers. He would rummage around in the dirt for scraps of lead and drop them into his tin can. One morning, Lead Face came out.

"Hey, there, watcha doin'?" it said.

"Lookin' for lead."

"How would you like some lead molds?"

"Hey, sure."

"Why don't you come back tomorrow around this time and I'll give you the molds," said Lead Face of Circle 7.

He returned the next day full of a child's expectation. Lead Face came out, his forehead and cheeks and beard streaked black with lead, and took him in the back and gave him a blowjob.

"He gave me a brown paper bag with three lead molds. It was disgusting. I never went back."

Shel Silverstein had to understand that his friend wanted to write about fucking his grammar school teacher, Susan Einway, because her greatest gift followed close upon the heels of Lead Face, a most propitious change to, instead of ever seeing Lead Face again, and in place of Sister in a black and white habit—here comes his substitute teacher in a clinging silk blouse, smelling great, and how he was all eyes as she removed her jacket, and it tickled him to see her pretty legs and her seams straight as arrows and the mole one-half inch from her lips, and then she raised the boards and took him by the hand back to the clothes closet.

Illustration, the Memoirs of Jacques Casanova, M. Blaine.

Never for a moment had he considered the jealousy, the profound unvoiced pain that Hef or any man who loved him experienced from watching him in Haley's mouth. Those same feelings that the handsome castrato called Bellino experienced as he watched the great lover Casanova make love to a Greek girl aboard a Turkish vessel, bound for Alexandria. Bellino—"handsome boy" in Italian—had asked Casanova if he could accompany him as far as Rimini, he had to sing in an opera after Easter. Bellino was Italy's "First Actress," a castrato singer 16 or 17 years of age who had had his testicles removed so that he could retain his beautiful, high-pitched soprano voice. The papacy forbade women with fine soprano voices to sing on stage so the castrati played the female roles. Casanova insisted that Bellino was, in truth, a woman, while (s)he insisted that (s)he was not. Scarcely stepping aboard the Spanish felucca, Bellino in tow, Casanova spots the beautiful Greek girl he had left behind seven months before. Dark and sultry, she stood beside the sea captain. Casanova being Casanova, he does not tell Bellino that he knows her and pretends not to notice the Greek girl, leaving any outward show of surprise and delight to her. He flatters the captain about some merchandise on sale so that he can forget momentarily his prized possession, who then whispers something to the captain, who leaves. Ignoring Bellino, she throws her arms around Casanova's neck and presses him to her breast.

"This is the happy moment," she says in Turkish, whereupon Casanova sits and guides her on top of him.

"In less than a minute," he writes in French, "I did for her what her master had not done once in seven years. I plucked the fruit and was eating it but to swallow it I needed one more minute."

All the while Bellino has been watching, frozen like a block of ice, his thin, curled lips parted slightly, trembling.

They drifted apart, he and Hef. He felt a growing indifference toward himself, dismissed, off radar. One who is indifferent does not recognize, see, hear. John does not say how this indifference was manifested. Placed beyond the rim of the inner circle? Surcease of invitations to functions, orgies? He could go away for ordinary days as well as holidays and not be missed. Or just a change in manners of speaking, soft friendly tone, a loving glance. John felt that he knew the cause.

"My obvious repugnance of the same-sex practice might have contributed to Hef's indifference to me, and it might have contributed to my starting to lose respect for him."

How could he respect a man who would violate another man who once had tremendous power and lost it, a man who had aroused the affection of thousands of the prime ladies and lost that, too. A man who had adopted the name of the greatest Italian poet who invented the modern Italian language and was now at a loss for words to describe how he felt. Hef had associated with this Italian long and deeply enough to know the supreme stature of an Italian's sense of respect—that there are no words to describe it, let alone its loss; that, for the Italian, respect is a state of being, a way of keeping the most innermost fears under wraps; that respect for others compensates for gaps in respect for oneself; and that such loss of respect carries with it disdain. His repugnance of the same-sex act was so deep-seated that, once he realized through the haze and euphoria of drugs that Haley was kissing him and he was still being sucked, and begged her, "Please, baby, please," an endearment Hef or any other man must have heard, to go back down and replace him so that he, John Dante, could regain muscle and heat, which the man not only could not do for him but could take away, returning this man to watching again, it abnegated any and all of the man's earlier feelings of desire for him and transformed to indifference. Never for a moment did he consider that, if it was Hef who sought to make love to him, he did so precisely *because* he had lost his power with its great aphrodisiac, precisely *because* Dante's Inferno burned down twice due to his integrity, precisely *because* he opted to carry his name without its nightclub, precisely *because* he was the one who told him, Hef, straight up, refusing to align himself with the Flatterers of Circle 8 Bolge 2 which are dipped in and out of excrement, nor with the Hypocrites lower down in Bolge 6, adorned in hooded cloaks bright gold on the outside, heavy lead on the inside, their step slow, agonizing. Hef had wanted to love pure, unadulterated him.

Courtesy John Dante, private collection

Time passed as the clock does. Not a word was said about the ménage-à-trois with Haley. It was like it never happened. Pleasing his friend Shel Silverstein, John doesn't write about Playboy down time. The compromise he struck for writing about his checkered yet interesting life outside of Playboy was to write only about the exciting times inside of it. Then one memorable night, Hef said, his indifference seemingly short-lived, willing to renew their relationship as it had been before:

"We're going to have a thing tonight."

"I think I'll pass," he said, and he went on to rebuff Hef as many times as he imagined he had let Hef do it to him.

"Hef got kind of miffed. After I turned him down several times, he said:

"'Look, John, I want you to know this—you are invited any time you want to come. No matter who or what it is, you are invited.'"

He began to hear echoes of the pragmatic side of his old self. He was 46 years old and still in pretty good shape. His parents continued on into their twilight years. Chef/philanthropist Noel Cunningham says that Maria Aimola kept a scrapbook of her son, empty pages waiting for good things to happen in Los Angeles. He was a high roller and loved to bet on the horses—well, Santa Anita and Hollywood Park race tracks were nearby, he could go with Don Adams, who came to play cards on Wednesday nights. Hef's unwavering love for him was giving him the time to rediscover his former prowess in new guises. Fresh business opportunities. Old friends Jimmy Caan and Tony Curtis had become international stars and were based right there in Los Angeles. Write a book and have a film made from it. Shel Silverstein made the transition from Chicago to Los Angeles with ease, equating his Mansion address with close friends Hef and John, staying awhile, long enough to take off his clothes in an orgy or two, according to John, then off to his new house in Key West or his apartment in lower Manhattan. Shel and Linda Lovelace had talked about collaborating on a country western music album—maybe he and Shel could collaborate on some sort of book. And new Bunnies and Playmates kept coming on to the scene, filling their house with youth and beauty and vigor. Was a lasting relationship still possible? Then Hef's persistence took a specific turn.

"We're having a thing tonight with Rachel Lee and a new girl."

He was proposing pairs: Hef-Rachel Lee/John-New Girl.

Suddenly, he felt *vita nuova*, new life.

"O.K.," he acceded.

THE SODOMITES

Gustav Doré, Lucifer. *Dante's Inferno.*

"Sodom, a plain which rejects all plants their seed."
—Dante Alighieri. *Inferno*, 16:46-47, the Sodomites

And then through the euphoria and jacuzzi vapors rising, John Dante hears, ' "How would you like to fuck me in the ass?' "

"Wooossshhh…" blow Hell's winds up from Circle 9, Hell's very last, produced by Lucifer's three pairs of wings that sprout from under his three heads, which are black, yellow, and vermillion. Satan or Beelzebub or Lucifer, call the devil what you will, has three salacious, drooling mouths which masticate but do not salivate. His appetite is endless—yet, he cannot digest his prey. This is the supreme contrapasso *of a once beautiful angel who had sought God's power and now reigns in Hell but cannot move, for the winds that his gigantic wings produce are so powerful that they freeze the ice that packs them. Six gigantic wings forever flapping, blowing, flapping, blowing—ssswwwooo… —driving upward Hell's shrieks and wails and laments. "How would you like to fuck me in the ass?" drifts up on Lucifer's powerful draft.*

The offer is strictly confidential, tendered in a whisper, meant for his, John's, ears alone. Naked, dripping wet, Rachel Lee and the New Girl turn to one another, smiling, pretending not to have heard.

He has at least two options. If, indeed, he heard the offer correctly, he could go ahead and fuck in the ass, while the women make love to the others down there and they them with their free hands and mouths and the one free fig. Agree to engage in anal intercourse as this orgy's epicenter, the woman surrounding and turning all their attention, watching from all angles in awe and appreciation, the way lesser dancers stop their dancing, stand aside, and watch the very best go at it in the center. Or, he could take guy aside and rebuff him, in a gentle, understanding manner. He doesn't have an eternity to respond.

THE DOWN SIDE

If Hef, his deep, mellifluous cry—"Aiiee! Aarrgh!"—must not be among the chorus of Sodomites who occupy Circle 3. His naked body must not be singed and smoked from the incessant falling flakes of fire. He must not be made to run forever as a way of keeping his bare feet off the burning sand. If Hef were among the Sodomites and stopped running even for a single moment of respite, he would have to lie for 100 years without brushing off the pelts of fire. Yes, keep running, but his head would be turned to the Sodomite running behind him, progressing ass backwards, forever looking into the baked face of a queer he doesn't know.

Hef, was it Hef? Perhaps the playboy he had always wanted to be which plateau he gained in Los Angeles amid the stars and a ratio of women to men 10 to 1, coming into the full realization of his power over young women, may have embraced experimenting with anal intercourse, which he now attempts to entrust, first and foremost, to his best friend, John Dante, so that later on, when and if he would invite, say, other men into the orgies like the Chippendale Dancers and porn stars and not John, he, John, would understand.

In the mid-1970s, three hundred thousand gay men were about to die from a nameless, sexually transmitted disease. International film star and romantic lead Rock Hudson would suffer another ten years in the proverbial closet. High profile celebrities like Mr. Hudson and Quentin Crisp and Liberace and Monty Clift could not easily join the thousands of gay men from around the world who migrated to San Francisco's Castro Street and New York City's Christopher Street so that they could stroll hand-in-hand in the open air, under the stars, stop, kiss, and cruise the gay establishments along the Hudson River. Could he or anyone even imagine Hef physically eroded, emaciated to the bone, riddled with lesions, without voice?

They could go to jail, as sodomy laws were still extant in California in the mid-1970s. Hef in pinstripe pajamas, confined to a 6x8-foot cell, sink, open toilet, and cot. "Voyeurs," peeping peace officers were called who spied on suspected sodomites through holes in walls or in paintings or in any orifice in which a camera could be inserted, the way Hard Boots spied on Linda Lovelace. If Hef had moved their house to, say, Idaho and such a voyeur captured them in *pedicavi coivi*—life imprisonment. To Michigan—15 years hard labor, Hef slinging a sledgehammer in a road gang. Founding Father Thomas Jefferson pulled back Virginia's law requiring the death penalty for buggery to castration, deciding that the majority of men, rather than face eternal pelts of fire and running on burning sand with their heads turned around, would opt for having their testicles removed and sprouting lovely alabaster breasts and retaining the high-pitched, lilting voice of their boyhood, like a castrati singer. If they had stayed in Chicago and were caught on camera, there would have been no penalty at all. In Chicago they had been free to bugger at will, their beloved state of Illinois being the first state to abolish sodomy laws in the early 1960s, around the time Hef purchased their first house. Later on, in the last hours of their erotic weekend, if Hef accompanied him to Florence, they would be free to practice anal sex, for, in Italy, anal sex between consenting adults—*vai avanti,* go right ahead!

If it were Hef, did he want him struck blind and turned to a pillar of salt like Lot's wife? As a safeguard against sodomy—that's why in hotel rooms across the United States one can find a bible. As the sun rose, night on the other side of the unknown world, the sand reflecting the color of the muted moon, "The Lord rained on Sodom and Gomorrah sulfur and fire…overthrowing these towns and the whole plain with all the inhabitants"—buggerers all. "But the wife of Lot looked back and was turned into a pillar of salt." Genesis 19:24-25 (English Standard Version). Upon turning, only Lot's wife saw, and forthwith was turned into salt like the salt of the oceans, which, then, washed down through the ages. Hef turned to a pillar of salt, like Lot's good, unnamed wife, if he, John Dante, responds in the affirmative.

What would Luigi and Petey and Tony and the Chicago gangsters think if they found out that their old paisan Johnny Dante was a fag? Hef or whoever it was had to understand that, in Italian neighborhoods, parents shipped their gay children out to seminaries and convents, and those who did not make it through returned home and shriveled and grew pale and sallow and sprouted sideburns and whiskers so that no one else save God would ever desire them. They donned white collars and black veils and became deacons and sub-deacons at their parish churches, ensuring that the vases of beautiful flowers that filled the churches with their sweet aromas were filled, and that, during the Lenten season, the statues of the saints were covered with purple cloth. His immigrant parents did not endure America's Great Depression wearing out their soles just to have their only son turn out to be a fag. Bad enough their paisans knew the kind of house the Aimola boy lived in and the kind of magazine he worked for, which you didn't even have to know English to read.

HEF AND BRUNETTO

"Is that you, Ser Brunetto?"
--Gustav Doré. *Inferno,* 16:46-47, the Sodomites

The night of their first day, Good Friday, is about to fall, and Dante and his guide Virgil are about to leave the pit of the Sodomites. They have made it through hastily, without incident. Virgil was chosen as Dante's guide because he had been a great classical poet, had written in Latin, as had Dante, and Virgil's CV states surprisingly, raising it as an issue: "He had homosexual leanings but did not act on them." The pilgrim and his guide scale a sandy dyke that banks the Phlegethon River, or River of Blood. Vapor rising from the river forms a canopy that protects them from the raining bolts of fire. Dante has come so far from his wood of error and sin that, if he were to turn back, he would not have regained his wood. He as well as his namesake John has reached the point of no return. Neither wants his head turned ass backward. Like John Dante for Hugh Hefner, Dante Alighieri does not want to be in the pit with the Sodomites. Daylight has faded to dusk, and a new moon shines in the sky as a band of Sodomites gambol along the burning sand. Being queer, they knit their brows at Dante and Virgil and glance up at them like the old tailor threading his needle. Then, a sharp tug at the hem of Dante's noble Florentine skirts. The Sodomites are approximately at the level of the poet's feet.

"How marvelous!" one bald, baked, prancing gay shade exclaims, and stretches out his arm to Dante, recognizing him from their halcyon days and nights in Florence. The shade can speak and be heard because of the love Dante had had for him, and because Dante's journey is also a tale and he wants to write something about this great man. Dante looks down in the direction of the pull on his skirts and stares at a beckoning shade's scorched face, searching through the shriveled skin and scarred features for identity.

"What, you here, Ser Latini? You?" for Bruno Latini had been an illustrious man and dedicated civil servant, renowned author and diplomat, notary and prior. Dante himself had called him, "A Radiance Among Men." And he'd had a wife and four kids. Dante had loved Brunetto, which means "baked," because he

taught him how to make things immortal by remembering and writing about them, because he had been the one man closest to him in the realm of loving another man in a corporeal way. Dante would not have Latini pull on his hem if he, Dante, had not loved him in a physical, though unrequited, way, had not felt in every fiber of his body that misdirected desire. Dante had rebuffed his teacher, who, then—and this is why Dante put him in Circle 7 Bolge 3—continued his homosexual ways.

"In your exile in France, you composed your encyclopedic work, Trésor, in French, raising the brows of advocators of the vernacular and vulgar tongue."

In the vulgar sense, Latini had fucked literary progress in the ass.

Had the young Dante known about his elder neighbor's and mentor's affairs in Spain and France?

THE UP SIDE

On the other hand, he had to consider that, for men like Hef, Shel, and himself, there would always be a procession of beautiful women, never just one, and so maybe Hef decided to make love to a single man he loved, his best friend, who, he hoped, would love him in return with affection, kiss him deeply and tenderly, and agree to have anal intercourse with him. For John Dante knew how to make anal sex. Here's the thing that he knew—you don't carry out anal intercourse the way dogs fornicate, from behind. In this second more positive scenario, the guy's virtual whisper, "How would you like to fuck me in the ass?" relaxes John's body, every muscle loses its tension and he feels joy, and a slight smile breaks over his wet face and moist eyes, which sparkle like stars. He goes over and takes by the hand and guides him gently on top of himself so that they are in a comfortable missionary position. They fit like a glove. Now they are eyes to eyes, nose to nose, mouth to mouth, around which play their respective warm breaths. Then, ever so imperceptibly, John slides his body down so that his partner is slightly higher, and then taps the side of a thigh, signaling spreading of the legs. Like an Italian totem, John's hard fig slices up between parted legs, then angles back and comes to rest at the threshold of the anus. It will enter only through their concerted effort.

If Hef, he had engineered such a position in their mortal lives so that his best friend could discern the humanity reflected in his face. John Dante will be able to say that, in their collective lifetimes, in their friendship of 40 years, he bore witness to Hugh M. Hefner's humanness. One person bore witness that, no matter the vicissitudes of life, sorrows and joys, throughout his long life Hugh Hefner remained constant to his raison d'être of personal and political freedom. That his life had been a confluence of fantasy and reality in that he had, for example, received into their house Elizabeth Taylor and Linda Lovelace and Clint Eastwood and Harry Reems with equal charm and grace. In Hef's hovering, loving face, his best friend, John, would see this constant supernumerary of fantasy and reality. And then he would press in his cock ever so slightly, so gently. Hef would grimace in initial pain and exhale a burst of stale air, but soon the pain would ease and his breathing return to normal, and now John is the one human being who glimpses vestiges of sorrow in Hef's eyes, the tears that well up. Hef's face reflects profound grief and sorrow over the deaths of Lenny Bruce and Bobbie Arnstein. John would enfold his arms around his grieving friend. His eyes set virtually against Hef's search them for a look of pity, for it is pity that the Suicides want.

LENNY BRUCE

Everybody knew that about Hef, John Dante claims, he was not receptive to downers, don't bring him bad news, manage yourself—still, bad news had a way of finding Hugh Hefner right away, often before anyone else. On a scorching hot day in August 1966, back in Chicago, somebody hands Hef the phone.

Lenny Bruce was found in the bathroom of his home (he had preceded Hef and John to Hollywood) naked, a bloody syringe and burned bottle cap at his side. The house has been cordoned off, and the death squad is in there now. His death has been termed "accidental" due to an overdose of drugs.

Lenny Bruce could do a bit—let's say at John Dante's Chez Paradisus—on the subject of his own demise.

" 'Accidental,' that's a fucking joke. I'd been aching for that extra gram for a lot of years. The fucking chronic wound of my soul was the way a human being suffers for being an innovative social commentator. I chose the fucking bathroom to die in so that my naked skin could abut on the cold bathroom tiles, where the air is diffused with the odors of piss and shit. In other words, ladies and gentlemen, I chose the toilet because the toilet is the one room in the house closest to Hell. That's it for now, folks, thank you, and thanks to John for having me and salutes to old friends out there in the audience—Linda and Shel and Bobbie and Dorothy and Noel, and back home especially to Hef for supporting me practically my whole fucking life."

Yes, they'd been friends from the early days in Chicago, after Hef dropped off a few copies of his new magazine and then he and John and Shel and Skippy and Frank went over to the Tradewinds or Milano's or the Cloister Inn in the basement of the Maryland Hotel to catch Lenny's act. The atmosphere of the lower levels of basement venues--the Cloister Inn as well as Smalls and the Village Vanguard in Greenwich Village, New York City, for example—seems conducive to the age's finest entertainment. Lenny Bruce had always been welcome in the Mansion, and he worked in Playboy clubs around the world, and toward the end of his earthly life, *Playboy* published his autobiography, *How to Talk Dirty and Influence People.*

Such a profound loss etched itself in a loved one's fabric, marrow. Tears well up in Hef's eyes, John can see.

BOBBIE ARNSTEIN

"Bobbie was harassed because they were trying to get to Hef. The attorney general or whoever the fuck it was trying to make a name for himself by getting to Hef."

"I Am the One Who Brought Down Hugh Hefner and the Playboy Empire."

To his dying day, John Dante was vehement in his defense of Hugh Hefner.

The time was toward the mid-1970s while Hef was deciding whether to move permanently to Los Angeles, and "whoever the fuck it was" was not the attorney general or state's attorney with gubernatorial ambitions. The picture was larger than that. Richard Nixon was president of the United States and transvestite J. Edgar Hoover was F.B.I. chief—shutting down Hefner and Playboy would be tantamount to catching Bonnie and Clyde and John Dillinger and opening diplomatic channels to China. Why, if Hefner's Sex Empire were not shut down, the Playboy Mansion could become a hoary retreat for repressed, high-profile individuals—presidents, governors, senators, athletes and actors, all with wayward libidos. Goddess knows, 3-D glasses would one day accompany your copy of *Playboy* sold on the newsstands so that our youth can view tits-and-ass in their proper perspective. Consider how much healthier our national moral and religious life would be without the filth and subversive humor emanating from the mouths of so-called comics whom Hef supports, like Red Foxx, Dick Gregory, Lenny Bruce, Irwin Corey, Mort Sahl, and George Carlin. How much richer our literary life without the inferior scribblings of the authors *Playboy* publishes, like Isaac B. Singer, Saul Bellow, Kurt Vonnegut Jr., Doris Lessing, John Updike, Joyce Carol Oates, John Cheever, James Dickey, Michael Crichton, John Le Carré, Commie poet Yevgeny Yevtushenko, and Nadine Gordimer. For the *Playboy* interviews, that *Roots* guy Alex Haley interviewed the upstart dissident Martin Luther King, Jr. and the subversive Malcolm X.

Once the decision was made to shut down Hefner and Playboy, what was needed was the means. Interstate phone sex originating from the Mansion?

"Hi."

"Oink."

"Aaahhhh..."

"Ooiinnnkkkk…."

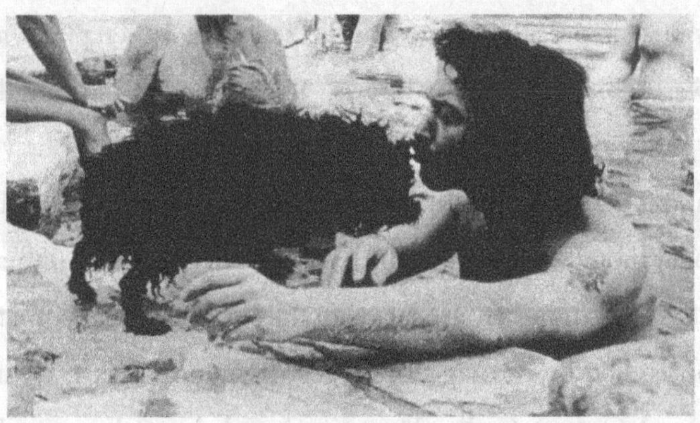

courtesy John Dante, private collection

The next step under law enforcement consideration was to place an undercover inside the Mansion. They must have a sexy woman on the force, dress her up as a cop all in leather and packing two guns for the Mansion Halloween Party. We can send in a chlorine inspector to demonstrate a new dye that turns purple if anyone pees in the Mansion swimming pool. There is this hanger-on who named himself after a famous Italian poet, Dante something, he hangs around the pool with his black poodle who is, allegedly, cocaine addicted. So just call out, "Looie! Looie!" and the mutt 'll come running, then say, "Give me a kiss, Looie," and he'll kiss your nose with a snout caked with cocaine.

Whoever the fuck it was decided to get Hefner on drug distribution charges. It was the Age of Methadone Maintenance, so junkies mixed their methadone with uppers and downers and alcohol. Cocaine was the illicit drug of the future. Tap the Mansion telephone, wait and see.

Lastly, they needed a go-between, a fall girl. There's this woman—of course, a woman!—who answers the Mansion telephone, Bobbie Arnstein, a Chicago native/Playboy lifer, straight out of high school into

Playboy, first as a Bunny then she took a desk job inside the Mansion as a secretary. Hefner made her an executive assistant with unlimited access to him. Listen to this—her boyfriend distributes cocaine.

In January 1975, based on wiretap evidence, Bobbie Arnstein was convicted of cocaine distribution and sentenced to 15 years in a federal prison. She told friends sardonically that she would not spend 15 minutes in prison. The F.B.I. offered her immunity in return for testifying against Hugh Hefner and Playboy, giving her the chance to take her life back and time to imagine herself living in a different sort of mansion: Alcatraz on the Rock, Sing-Sing on the Hudson. Let her picture herself for 5,475 days and nights in pinstripe pajamas, elbow to elbow with violent, vindictive women, a woman among other women at the mercy of their rapacious jailers. Only to conclude—Hef go to jail instead of me, Hef don the black-and-white pinstripe pajamas instead of me.

While free on bond, awaiting appeal, Bobbie Arnstein learned that a grand jury investigating alleged Playboy drug distribution was about to subpoena her. The following tactic, intended to take her over the top and have her testify against Hefner, would guarantee a governorship, second presidential term, founding of a new religious order. She is called into a federal office and told that they had conclusive evidence from two independent reliable sources that her employer, Hugh Hefner of Playboy Enterprises, put out a contract on her life in order to keep her from testifying before the grand jury. Her option of turning state's evidence was still open.

Had the hit gone through the Chicago Outfit? Imagine Hef giving Momo Giancana the Kiss of Death, flush on the lips? Giancana had also been scheduled to appear before a Senate committee investigating alleged collusion between the C.I.A. and the M.A.F.I.A. in a plot to assassinate President John F. Kennedy. One night before his scheduled appearance, Momo is frying the best Italian sausages in the world, made right there in Chicago, in the basement of his home. It is in the cool, dark basement of their homes, the black of their chiaroscuro, where Italians conduct the business of their lives. A crony stops by, so the boss puts in another couple of links. Whoever the fuck it was, most likely in mid-conversation, gets up, revolver drawn, creeps up behind the back of Momo Giancana, and fires a shot through his head, splattering his brains over the top of his stove. As his *contrapasso*, the punishment that suits his sins, Giancana's assassin turns him over so that his last image is the face of his assassin who betrayed their blood bond and trusted friendship, a fellow made man, a paisan. This person, who has yet to be found, shows the dying man the gun that killed him and then fires another shot straight into his face, then another into his neck, still another in his face—until six more bullets pump into him.

The Maryland Hotel was once an elegant hotel. Built in 1928, when Hef was two years old in Chicago and John was born across the ocean in Italy, the Maryland had 300 first-class rooms, a five-star restaurant, a drugstore and, in the basement, the famous Cloister Inn, where they all used to go after Dante's Inferno closed to catch the great performers at the 2 o'clock show. Duke Ellington and Ramsey Lewis and their bands. Buddy Rich of Brooklyn, New York brewed up a percussive storm. Della Reese, Bobby Short, and Anita O'Day filled the air with their stylish voices, and Dizzy Gillespie blew the first sounds of bebop. But then new hotels went up with larger, cheaper rooms, and the Cloister Inn became the Celebrity Lounge devoid of celebrities, and then transformed to a go-go lounge, featuring half-clad, tree-swinging girls. The Maryland's rooms fell into disrepair, and no one of any note stayed there. It had become a mere shell of itself with fond memories. On a bitter cold January night in 1975, it was a good place to die.

John sees in Hef's pitying eyes that, while he had been enjoying his new sweet life in the warm waning afternoon of Los Angeles, their good friend and colleague Bobbie leaves a dinner party hosted by friends and is beset by a wave of loneliness and desolation. She detours from the route to the Mansion, the only home she has known in her adult life, and heads a few blocks north toward the Maryland Hotel. She goes in and signs the register under an assumed name, as she had been a habitué of the place, seen with certain famous men. She drops the door key and her coat and pocketbook on the bed and spills out handfuls of barbiturates, sleeping pills, and Valium. She goes to the window on the south face and looks out at the freezing darkness. The shades of John and Hef appear on either side of her, and all three look out a few blocks south toward their house and the icy darkness and dead silence, and the terrible time of men pressing in transforms to a solitary moment of peace, warmth, and light. Some of her last thoughts had been of Hef. She left a note:

"My immediate employer, Hugh Hefner, showed courage, perhaps to his detriment, tho I hope not, and the kind of loyalty for which I hope—even as I write this—he is not wrongfully punished…I am innocent…despite the perjured testimony of the government's star witness, I was never part of any conspiracy to transport or distribute the alleged drugs connected with this case."

The shade Loyal Friend drops with a thud in Hell's Forest of the Suicides, Circle 7 Bolge 2, and then Loyal Friend sprouts like a grain of wheat and, instantly, grows into a shoot and then a wood plant. If Hef and John were traveling with the pilgrim Dante and his guide Virgil and they entered the Forest of the Suicides, they would see a wood with dark trees that bear no fruit and have knotted, twisted, poisonous thorns and, nestled in these trees, the Harpies, half-bird/half-women preying beasts with broad wings and sharp, crooked claws and feathered bellies, human faces and necks, who feed and tear and masticate on Suicide Trees' leaves, which is the only sound in this forest. They would see that everything about a Harpie—pointed beak, clawed feet, hairy breasts—is antithetical to all that a playboy desires in a woman. The half-woman/half-bird Harpie could have been another hybrid beast that the select few morphed into in the Mansion Bath House as they watched the large dog Rufus attempt to fuck Linda Lovelace. One of the travelers, Hef or John, brushes the wood plant Loyal Friend, causing it to break off and bleed, and lament:

"I am she who kept faith to her office. My spirit, believing by death to liberate my loved ones from torment, made me unjust against my just self."

Then Loyal Friend breaks into poetry of her own:

I was once a Playboy Bunny
High heels and rabbit ears my costume.
O yeah could I be funny,
Passing glassine bags in the courtroom.
Of unwarranted lovers and blinding drugs my strife
My song Shel plays forever on his fife."

Well, John Dante, the pros and cons are in. The scale is balanced. Are you or are you not going to fuck Hef or whoever the fuck is there, in the ass? Here is what he decides to do—nothing.

"I pretended not to hear."

Thus far in his two centerpiece orgies, with the third remaining on the Sunday evening of his one weekend of ecstasy, in the first he did not see and in the second he did not hear. The truth according to John Dante may be a reverie. Or the pain he experienced at the time and in his memory was simply too severe, the turn of events incredible and heartbreaking so his response of pretending not to hear spared both Hef and himself falling tongues of fire that burn and rip the skin, running forever on burning sand, and looking back over their shoulders at gamboling strange queers. After he pretended not to hear, their eyes unlocked, his and Hef's, and their wet, tense bodies, frozen in that instant of call and response, animated once again, as did those of Rachel Lee and the New Girl, and they continued on with great carnal pleasure.

THE TOUCH CLUB

As a result of his wise action of waiting for the world to turn ever so imperceptibly before responding whether or not he would fuck the man in the ass, and then pretending not to hear so that only he and perhaps Hef would be the only two persons in history to know and to suffer their consciences and memories, each in their own way—molecule by molecule, atom by atom, John Dante returned fully to himself. The shade of him reclaimed its full corporeal presence, with a smile, emoting Je Reviens perfume, and dancing, hands and cheeks touching. He was once again proprietor of one of Chicago's most innovative nightclubs who refused twice to traffic in prostitution, once again a man of impeccable taste and eye who interviewed 20,000 stunning women in mesh stockings and high heels, the man who facilitated the twin-city romances of his best friend via management of the Playboy jet. Once again, John Dante had a future on planet Earth. In all likelihood, Hef knew all this, at least that John was a good man and a good friend, one of the very few who told him straight up.

"At that time Hef loved me, and he understood my need to do something meaningful in order to revive my self-esteem that had eroded since I quit my job [with Playboy]."

That time was the approach of the 1980s, and Hef, John, and Shel were in their 50s, and Hef loved John and knew full well his brilliance and genius in the nightclub and restaurant business. As a result, the best of friends for about 25 years then, housemates for 10 of those years, rounded their relationship by becoming business partners in a supper club. Hef would finance it and John would set up and manage the finest private supper club the people of Los Angeles had ever seen or heard about. Unlike the bygone, glorious salad days of Chicago, peering though the grimy window of a dilapidated mom and pop grocery store near Skid Row, money was no object. Hef invested $4.5 million.

"I owned 49%. Hef would never give up full or equal control of anything. This I understood."

He named their club "Touch," which he came to from its opposite. At the parties Hef used to throw in the Chicago Mansion when he was newly hired and had never seen anything like them in his life with Bunnies, Playmates, and models in party attire and frames of mind and the Harold Harris quintet played—well, Chubby Checker also performed the Twist:

"Come on, baby, let's do the Twist…"

He hated the dance because couples danced—swiveled!—apart, as if alone, while he loved dancing where couples touched, pressing one into the other the warmth of their arms and hands and face, like the foxtrot, two-step, waltz, and tango—suddenly, the bandoneón which sounds like an accordion plays the tango's first aching note, and Hef approaches and reaches out his hand, which John grasps and then, arms around waists, they step and slide and pull up close. In the touching tango, the man leads—Hef and John take turns leading. Originally, the tango was the dance of two men in the bordellos of Buenos Aires while they waited their turns with the women who were busy. Of the tango, the great Argentine writer Jorge Luis Borges wrote:

"The tango can be debated, and we have debates over it, but it still encloses, as does all that is truthful, a secret."

Their tangoan secret, Hef and John's, is that they love one another.

I Was The One Who Loved Hugh Hefner.

I Was the One Who Loved John Dante.

The plaque that he put up on Touch's front door was of a couple dancing in the style of the 1930s, the guy in a top hat a la Fred Astaire, the girl with golden curls a la Ginger Rogers, their bodies in graceful sync, as if to say that, no matter the dismal black and white world of America's Great Depression, we can make it through together, touching, derive solace and warmth and style through the touching of our bodies and, through them, our souls.

Noel Cunningham—"I opened and closed Touch with John"—presents a positive view about how Touch came into being other than the one about Hef seeking to elevate John's sense of poor self-esteem.

"You could say that John was bored with his life in Los Angeles during the waning years of the '70s and Hef wanted to give him a plaything and Hef wanted to bolster John's self-esteem—but the truth is that John knew that Playboy's days were numbered and he had a vision called Touch, a franchise of the finest private supper clubs around the country and then the world, that would propel Playboy and, hence, his friend into the modern age."

At its height, according to John Dante, Playboy had 22 clubs employing more than 25,000 Bunnies, and the clubs boasted more than a million key holders, or members. But then, beginning in the mid-1970s, one by one, like the light of the chiaroscuro turning dark, Playboy clubs in key cities—San Francisco, Denver, Kansas City—began to lose money or shut down.

"The closing of the Atlantic City casino hit Playboy Enterprises extraordinarily hard," states Noel Cunningham. "And the Los Angeles, New York, and Chicago Clubs were barely making stand-alone profits."

John writes:

"I was there for Playboy's near collapse with the closing of the London casino."

For awhile, the London Playboy Club and Casino, 80 betting shops and six bingo parlours and three additional casinos in Britain more than compensated for the aforementioned losses and closings. One may find Hugh Hefner's venturing into the casino business interesting in the sense that he was not about to take his card game losses to old friends Don Adams and Shelly Kasten lightly. He would turn things around in the broad sense with profits from gambling losses of players from around the world. Lit brightly by the crystal chandeliers of London's Park Lane establishment, Playboy Bunnies in enticing costume and sharp, made-up eyes and cultivated, sinuous hands spun the roulette wheels and dealt the cards and raked in the millions laid down by the world's oil czars. A seemingly endless supply of oil mirrored the endless supply of money siphoned into Playboy's coffers. It was a major stroke of irony, then, that heavy losses at the gaming tables contributed to Playboy's near collapse in that they lead to requests for credit, which Playboy issued, and bad checks were written and taken, accounts settled later on. As long as there was oil in the earth, the debts would be made good. A committee of four magistrates in powdered wigs and faces and glad hearts heard evidence, including from one sheik who had cashed around $4 million worth of checks drawn on more than a dozen banks that were returned unpaid and eventually made good. Unlike John Dante now, British gaming laws reserved little faith in the future. Clement Freud, grandson of Sigmund Freud and a member of Parliament then, was allowed to try his luck at the gaming tables while serving as a Playboy director. The Magistrates frowned on this conflict of interest, unwilling to bestow privilege on a direct descendant of the famous psychiatrist. Two witnesses acknowledged that they had been paid to testify against Playboy by a rival casino operator. Also, one character acted as a go-between by steering uber-rich men and women to Playboy's tables and to the Bunnies. The magistrates feasted their eyes and listened to former Bunnies testify about how this go-between brokered liaisons, coming into the casino with a fistful of cash held aloft, shouting:

"Lots of monies to spend on Bunnies!"

The magistrates caucused. As a show of good faith, Playboy fired Victor Lownes, head of gaming operations in London and Hefner's long-time friend, to whom John Dante mistakenly extended his hand all those years ago in Chicago, in his club Dante's Inferno on Opening Night with snowflakes the size of quarters falling and Renée called up, "Hef is here," and John went down—that was Victor Lownes to whom he had extended his hand, the wrong guy of the two who looked the part of a playboy: tall, handsome, wearing a sharp black mohair suit, Hef standing aside, amused. The magistrates ruled against Playboy. Its casinos and betting and bingo parlours were shut down. The adverse ruling affected the Atlantic City Gaming commission's ruling whether or not to grant Playboy a license to operate its already built $150 million casino. Hef appeared before the gaming commission, promising to alter Playboy's image, alas, get rid of the rabbit ears, and hire male Bunnies for the New York Playboy Club. To no avail, and the Atlantic City gaming license was not granted.

John witnessed the terrible toll all of this had on his friend. It was then that he decided to act on his idea of a franchise of stylish private supper clubs called Touch. States Noel Cunningham:

"John designed Touch to transform Playboy's waning life into a modern version of itself, and, in the process, help sustain and transform his good friend Hef."

John found a prime location in Beverly Hills and put out a call for a chef. A chef from Ireland answered the ad.

Noel Cunningham was born in Dublin, Ireland of a father and uncle who were chefs and a mother who was a waitress. Thus, his family sought to steer him away from the food business. Feeling that his curved back and rounded shoulders were abnormal, Noel's parents sent the 13-year-old to a stay-in orthopedic hospital, where his mates suffered with horrible physical and congenital deformities. Noel says:

"It was hard for them, and living with them made me see how much it hurt. It hurt me, too, to know how they felt."

Noel ran away with a buddy who had two fingers coming out of where his arms and shoulders should have been. He also ran away from the next Christian school his parents placed him in—thus, Noel and John Dante have running away in common. Noel was deemed incorrigible and, lest he end up in jail or worse, his father and uncle put him to work in their restaurant. It was Hell, a great place to apprentice.

"My father smacked me around because he didn't want anyone to think he was showing favoritism."

At the age of 17, Noel managed to get away from his father's beatings by taking a job at the famous Savoy Hotel in London and then, at the age of 23, became the youngest sous chef that London's Berkeley Hotel ever had. The future looked brighter, and he married and had children. In 1976, on the occasion of the United States' bicentennial celebrations, Noel and his family visited Disneyland, and stayed. He departed from his Hell in England and would soon find an American version in the state of California. He became chef at the Hermitage and the Chianti. Then he answered a call for top chef at a new private supper club in Beverly Hills called Touch. He sat across from a character who called himself John Dante.

"What is your recipe for Veal Chop Riesens?" this Dante asks.

"I don't know how to make Veal Chop Riesens," Noel Cunningham responds. "But I do know how to make a first-rate veal chop dish. Prime veal with herbs and garnish..."

"You're hired—" Dante interrupts. "And I'll tell you why. Because you're not a bullshitter. There is no recipe for Veal Chop Riesens. Riesens is the name of a friend of mine after whom I want to name a veal dish."

John put Noel on the payroll months before Touch's opening night. Says Noel:

"John took Hef's money very seriously. He checked each and every invoice. He went to a Palm Tree farm and bought our trees and set them in and designed them so that two bottom stalks stuck out and touched. I remember in the kitchen there was a long black counter with a cover, and a plug ran behind and down along the floor and had to be plugged in. John couldn't reach the fucking plug. The electrician was standing there. 'You mean, I have to pay for a plug I can't reach?' John looked around. 'Didn't anybody catch this in the plans?' "

John designed the dance floor in the shape of a half-moon so that when you were dancing, touching, it was like you were dancing outside under the firmament filled with shooting stars and the moon in changing phases. The candescent ceiling and wall lighting were "amazing," says Noel. "He had a mahogany Lazy Susan hand-carved for the caviar server." A chiaroscuro marble floor was set in. Touch would seat 120, and members would sit on the finest chairs the proprietor could find, for which he paid $500 each. As for staff, Noel states:

"He hired waiters for the dining room and cocktail waitress for the bar and dance floor. He told us that no matter how rich and famous our patrons would be, we should touch each one on a personal level. He also told us he would not tolerate anyone who treated staff in an inappropriate manner. I remember when he was interviewing for cocktail waitresses. He hired a short girl and a tall one and women of color and Asian women, but then he didn't hire this knockout. I said, 'Hey, John, what the fuck?' He said, 'Baskin Robbins has umpteenth varieties of ice cream because not everybody eats vanilla.' "

Opening Night approached. Spiffy staff in place, menu of Veal Chop Riesens, steak, lobster, local vegetables and fruits and crepes, caviar and champagne. Once again, just like for the opening of the Welcome Inn in northern Wisconsin and the opening of Dante's Inferno, he got the jitters. He postponed Opening Night and postponed a second and third time. With the approach of yet another Opening Night, someone close to him made up the plausible story that, if they did not open this time, they would lose their liquor license. Touch's final Opening Night arrived, and he shut his office door behind him. Around 7 o'clock, Noel peeked in:

"John, 27 Rolls-Royces are parked in the parking lot, and each one carried at least two people."

Moguls of the film and music business, studio heads, and William Morris agents came. Mega movie stars Sophia Loren, Michael Caine, and Lucille Ball sat down to dinner. In time, members brought in other members. To become a member of Touch, you had to be brought in by an existing member. In this way, you could spend an evening with persons you know and like, and touch. The Frank D'Rone trio came in from Chicago. On the occasion of the birthday of producer Aaron Spelling's (The Mod Squad, Charlie's Angels) daughter, Michael Jackson turned up and sang and danced. When Shel Silverstein was in Los Angeles and staying at the Mansion, he frequented his friend's new place.

"John's Touch club was the finest supper club I've ever been in," Shel had told me.

Noel Cunningham observed the friendship.

"You could see how close Shel and John were. The respect they had for each other."

One night, a patron kept sending her steak back to the kitchen. "I was really mad. I took it personally," Noel Cunningham recalls. "John told me to calm down and to call him when the steak was ready again, which I did. He took the dish out and said to her, 'I'm going to shove this down your fucken' throat piece by piece.' "

Coinciding with the birth of John's vision of Playboy's future called Touch was the tragedy of Dorothy Stratten.

One lovely summer day that could only be matched by the wholesomeness and exquisite beauty of Dorothy Stratten herself, a car with Canadian license plates pulls up to the Playboy Mansion, and she steps out into the golden light.

"I was there on that sunny afternoon when she arrived. She was wide-eyed, beautiful, naïve."

John recalls a quiet, uneventful morning with her in the Mansion.

"Dorothy and I were having breakfast—"he was sitting directly across from her—"when we heard Hef coming down the stairs from his quarters to join us, coughing."

The padrone's coughs, like trumpet fanfare, announces his imminent arrival.

The Most Beautiful was discovered working in a Dairy Queen in Ontario, Canada, by a shade called Soft Ice Cream, who is up to his eyes in Hell's River of Blood for Murderers, Circle 7 Bolge 1. He pursued her and opened her to the reality and potentiality of sex, and then parlayed her generosity into allowing him to photograph her, which photos he sent to Hugh Hefner so she could meet his eyes, then the world's. But Soft Ice Cream did not want another man to desire Dorothy Stratten other than from the photographs he took of her. He could not have foretold the wide-ranging ramifications of the world of Hugh Hefner and John Dante, the Playboy world, and the rich and the famous she would meet. Pure and simple, Soft Ice Cream was—

"... a hustler and a pimp."

Everyone who saw her with him could see that, before he wallowed up to his eyes in viscous blood, he was a hustler and a pimp. But she was the one who knew him, the one who was intimate with him. She may have been unfaithful to him late one silent night in the Mansion Jacuzzi, and then she became the Murderer's wife and, at a Mansion party, met an esteemed young director, and they fell in love. Her talent as an actress was about to be exhibited to the world. What about him—what could he progress to? He would always be the one who discovered Dorothy Stratten in a Dairy Queen. He wasn't even real ice cream. He was soft.

"And I was in the Game House two years later playing pinball with Hef and others around midnight when the call came that she'd been murdered."

Once again, tragic news reached Hef almost immediately. First, on June 25, 1966, the call from Los Angeles while police cordoned off Lenny Bruce's house, the police photographer taking shots of the great stand-up comedian white as a ghost, lying naked on the cold tiles, his pants down around his ankles, a bloody syringe and burned bottle cap at his side. Then, on January 20, 1975, the call from Chicago about Bobbie Arnstein, found dead of a drug overdose in a top-floor room of the decaying Maryland Hotel. Now, August 14, 1980, the terrible news reached Hef while he was playing in the Game House with John. Hef is handed the phone.

Dorothy is dead. Murdered earlier that day by the hustler/pimp who then turned the shotgun on himself and blew his head off. Their naked, shot-up bodies were found in his bedroom. Soft Ice Cream had bought a .38 caliber pistol, then, from an ad in the personals, a $200, hand-pumped Mossberg 12-gauge shotgun, which its seller showed him how to use. Then it was just a question of finding the right moment. Around noon that hot August afternoon, Dorothy had gone over to 10881 Clarkson to placate him, end their marriage in an amicable way, and give him money. A large amount of cash was found in the bedroom. She had bought him a Mercedes Benz on which he installed the license plate Star 80. High on drugs, mad with jealousy, he fastened her to a workout/bondage bench that was found beside the bed. He had been trying in vain to sell the bench to the porno industry—a 2' x 6' piece of plywood with loops, straps, and bolts. Then he raped her. After that, he turned her over and sodomized her, nearly tearing her body apart. Then he took out the shotgun which he had hidden. It was the kind of shotgun you had to hold and aim on your shoulder, and he aimed the cold end of the smooth 18 1/2-inch barrel practically onto her left cheek and then, in a frenzy, his right forefinger pressed the trigger—one 2 3/4-inch shell blew off the left side of her face, killing her instantly. One load of buckshot released and scattered 20 lead pellets, of which one tore off her left pinkie. The time of her death was estimated at 1 p.m. For the next hour, he had sex on her corpse, including anal intercourse. His bloody handprints were found on her buttocks. At approximately 2 o'clock, he turned the hand-pumping shotgun on himself, between his eyes, and fortuitously had enough strength to pull the trigger. His body was found beside the bed, the face blown away, one eye hanging out of its socket.

In her most intimate moments with her killer, in their most intense throes of sexual ecstasy, she may have divined his capacity for extreme violence, even murder, and so she may have decided to end her story by submitting to his violence. She could not have foretold that he would then kill himself and become a tree in the Wood of Suicides, in the same godforsaken forest as loyal Bobbie Arnstein. Soft Ice Cream's contrapasso is to spend all eternity alternating between immersion up to his eyes in the River of Blood and being masticated by the nesting half-bird, half-woman Harpies in the Wood of Suicides.

Dorothy Stratten's remains rest in Westwood Village, Los Angeles, in an area of celebrities that includes the gravesite of Marilyn Monroe, beside which Hugh Hefner, purportedly, will rest in peace. Dorothy Stratten's gravestone is flat so that her burial place on sacred ground is contiguous with the surrounding nature of Palm Trees and roses, and it is perpetually adorned with freshly cut flowers. Her epitaph taken from *A Farewell to Arms* by Ernest Hemingway, who himself is a tree in the Forest of Suicides, reads as follows:

"If people bring so much courage to this world the world has to kill them to break them, so of course it kills them…It kills the very good and the very gentle and the very brave impartially. If you're none of these you can be sure that it will kill you too but there will be no special hurry."

Grieved Angel. Protestant cemetery, Rome.
Photo by Anthony Valerio

By the end of the first year, Touch had 300 members, one of whom was Joanna Carson, wife of the late-night talk show host Johnny Carson. According to Noel Cunningham, it amused John to no end that the Carsons' divorce settlement required that she receive thousands of dollars for flowers.

"John said, 'I'm going to take another look at this broad.' Another night he's by the dance floor with friends and Joanna comes over and tells him, "John, we're short of chairs," and he replies in the vulgar tongue, 'You want me to shit a fucken chair?' "

He cared for their Touch club. It touched him to the core. It was his *capolavoro,* his Sistine Chapel. Every day he came in through the back door and checked that the trash had been taken care of and that the ice machine was filled. He loved it there so much, says Noel, "that he didn't want to go home to the Mansion."

But then the unforeseen and, at the same time, the most natural phenomenon in life occurred, and it shocked him.

"I knew that a radical change would occur when one of my parents died. One of my nightmares was that I'd get a call that either my father or my mother was dying, and now the responsibility of the remaining parent would fall to me and I didn't know how to handle it. I figured that my mother would survive my father and, if that were the case, it wouldn't be too bad, because my mother was strong."

From the time of the Black Death, women in general have post-deceased men, maybe, like John says, because women are stronger. It was the diminutive Italian woman Maria Aimola who carried her son in steerage and through the meat factory of Ellis Island, racing through the great metropolis to catch the train to Chicago because the poet she had allowed to love her could not afford the ticket to New York, then they took a bus to a walk-up flat. It was his mother who found gainful employment in America during its Great Depression at the Marshal Laundry with "a little Jewish man, Mr. Berman," who showed her how to handle money and buy real estate, how to put money down and have the place pay for itself with tenants. And it was Maria Aimola who paid the bills and placed nourishing, palatable food on the table—vegetables, baccala—so that her Giovanni, the *giovanotto* who had accompanied her from the old world, could grow big and strong. But it was she who predeceased her husband. He flew back to Chicago.

"My mother left an estate of $600,000—$45,000 in cash in a brown paper bag for me, a three-story apartment building valued at $225,000 with 7 flats, and 10 acres of land outside Chicago that somebody wanted to give me $150,000 for in '85 and so I didn't sell."

He placed his father in a nursing home in Chicago, then returned to his life in the Mansion and at Touch. Promptly, he acquired a cocaine habit. He worried about his father. After work, hyped up, filled with guilt in addition to worry, he could not sleep. So he brought his father out to Los Angeles and placed him in a nursing home out where the sun sang, like in Fossacesia, which had a way of exacerbating his son's sense of guilt.

"Just to visit him every two days made me feel bad throughout the week. I tried to figure out how to relieve myself of the guilt."

He felt guilt "over being the one chosen to lead the life of a playboy for over 40 years." On top of this guilt lay the guilt of not caring for his father in an adequate manner, this despite the fact that the man had administered beatings to him that "today would be considered child abuse." Nothing he had accomplished in his life, nothing his good friends could tell him assuaged his overall sense of guilt. Guilt deafened and blinded him. Guilt was not unlike the power he once wielded—he wore both like a stolen silk suit. They were the mortar of a multi-level house of cards. Time and again, Hef told him, to no avail:

"It's OK, John. Don't worry about it."

He had to spend more time with his father, not a couple of hours a week in his nursing home, but solid time, the way mother, father, and son had lived together in a conventional home. So he bought such a conventional home, in Taos, New Mexico, and his father consented to live with him a couple of months out of the year. He told Hef—

"—and he flipped. 'What do you owe your father?' Hef said." Perhaps Hef knew about the beatings. He continued, " 'You owe me!' "

Says Noel Cunningham, "Hef didn't understand that it was only a couple of months for two or three years. John's father wanted to die and be with his wife."

Hef was supposed to understand that John's commitment to his father was short-termed and that he, Hef, should try to get through life without John for the two years or so that it would take Aimola to join his wife in Paradise.

He made arrangements for Touch to go on without him for awhile, took his father out of the nursing home, and together they went to live in the new house in Taos, New Mexico.

Hef had to understand also that John was relating to his father the way his beloved mother would have. She would never have placed him in a nursing home, let alone leave him there. Home is sanctuary, like church, and allowing a family member to go to a nursing home tended by strangers, or even a hospital with still more strangers—Italians of her generation just didn't do that, it was an *infamnia,* a disgrace. It meant that the family, the bulwark of Italian life, didn't care enough. So powerful a person was John's father in his life that he does not name him in his notes. "My father" is all. He learned about the man's early life from his mother.

"Once, he possessed the heart of a poet," she told him.

AIMOLA

Born in 1903 in the mountain town of Fossacesia—"a dreamily serene little town on the Adriatic"—province of Abruzzo, celebrated for its fine wines and extra-virgin olive oil, Aimola was the eldest of a poor family of 13. He dropped out of high school and, instead of working the family farm and helping out with the siblings, hung out at the Chieti Bar, located off the Piazza di San Giovanni, and cruised for the town's beauties. That's how a poet's heart works!—yearns for that one soaring subject of his poetry, his muse, his Beatrice. One day—there she is! on the evening stroll with her parents in the spring day's waning golden sunlight. Can't be more than 14 years old—perfect!—short but robust, and, even from afar, Aimola could see her eyes glittering like stars. It was *amore al primo colpo*, love at first sight. Having nothing else to do, Aimola followed her everywhere, at times capturing her attention, whereupon he smiled, exhibiting in his eyes and around his mouth the bright rays of his poetic heart. He gestured wildly with his arms, like a clown, by way of informing her that, despite the rigors of life, he owned enough of a sense of humor to get them through. He proclaimed from across the piazza:

"I love you! I want to marry you!"

Her father—"a fierce, very ill-tempered man"—chaperoned her everywhere.

"He was a crimp in her parents' lofty ambitions for her, their bargaining chip for elevating their backward, ambitious social status."

Maria's parents reminded her constantly of what a loser Aimola was. They attempted to bolster her flagging self-esteem by introducing her to families with sons who would become fishermen with their own boats and olive grove owners with their own *agriturismo* restaurants. One beautiful spring night, the deep azure sky studded with silver stars and a bright sickle moon, Aimola comes beneath her window with his mandolin, and begins singing the popular serenade, "You Are the Most Beautiful."

Tu sei la piu' bella
tu sei la mia stella…
You are the most beautiful
You are my star…

Her French doors swing open. Maria comes onto her balcony, smiling coquettishly, at the same time waving him away. Her father hides in her bedroom shadows. Aimola's voice and mandolin soar—

Tu sei mio amore
insieme con te staro'

Her father emerges into the moonbeams shining on the balcony.

"I'll kill you! She's only 14!"

He called a meeting at the parish church, which was packed with families of violated young women.

"A hectare of olive trees for the child molester's head!" the father pontificated.

So Aimola went into hiding, and Maria looked for him around the piazza, their church, out in the vineyards. His forced absence lured her to him more than ever. He sends her word of his whereabouts. She climbs down from her balcony window on a foggy night.

"After all, what woman can resist the sustained passion of an obsessed troubadour?"

She finds him in his secret cache in a hillside vineyard. They make love on the soft burlap between rows of vines, in the dappled sunlight, then under the stars. A child is conceived.

The carabinieri scour the safe havens of the abbey and cloister of San Giovanni, the hills between the Adriatic and Maiella mountains. But, like the eel that he is, Aimola manages to slither from the grasp not only of the vigilantes after his scalp and her crazy family and the town of Fossacesia and province of Abruzzo--but all of Italy! He takes ship for America. Better a maligned alive Italian in America than a brave dead one in Italy. Aimola was one of the fortunate ones with relatives in America. From 1903 to 1924, around the time of his passage, 50 Aimolas emigrated from Italy to the United Sates, 14 from the town of Fossacesia. Passing through Ellis Island, this Aimola boards the Twentieth Century Limited at Grand Central Station, New York City, destination Chicago.

His mother returned to her family in disgrace. He gestated in her womb, while his father tried to raise the money for their passage in Chicago. The disgrace on the Italian side intensified. If they didn't kill her already, why kill her now? Kill daughter, kill grandchild. Place baby in covered basket on church doorstep and force her into the nunnery or a bordello, as prostitution was legal in Italy until the end of World War II.

Giovanni Aimola, a.k.a. John Dante, courtesy John Dante
Private collection

After three months in Taos with his father, he returned to Los Angeles and placed his father back in the nursing home. John provides no information about the quality of time with his father in Taos, how long they stayed, what the house was like. It existed only in the context of his guilt. There was no abode on earth for John Dante except the Playboy Mansion. According Noel Cunningham, Hef had issued an ultimatum to John: Taos and your father or me—still, Hef took John back. It seems that there was nothing John could do under the sun that would cause Hef to tell him to leave. That was one extent of his love for John.

Aimola had still not joined his wife in Paradise, and their son's sense of guilt amplified. He started doing more cocaine than before he'd left, and, after work at Touch—

"I'd be hyped up and couldn't fall asleep. I wanted somebody there." Private scenes and communal orgies no longer sufficed. "I started doing hookers because I didn't want the responsibility of an affair." He had descended from the woman of a marriage to the woman of an orgy to the woman of an affair to a working woman. "I met this woman Terry, and she sent me first-timers because she knew I was gentle and would respect the girls and they would have a good time."

"Somebody there," and that somebody had to be a woman, and from the thousands of women he'd made love to whose careers he had helped along, he could not call on a single one to keep him company without feeling that she expected something in return. Not a single woman to maybe go with him to visit his father in the nursing home or listen to him patiently talk about Hef's possessiveness, which, along with his cocaine use, seemed on the increase. He had had some fleeting good luck with first-timers, like the one in the Welcome Inn who, on his birthday, no longer a first-timer, gave him a watch. Had he sunk so low that he would seek to impress women whose company he paid for? "Really, you owned a nightclub modeled after Hell?" "You know James Caan and Warren Beatty and Tony Curtis—and Hef! "Sure, we'd love to participate in an orgy or two. What's the going rate?" That would be better than passing Hef in the hallway or glimpsing him through the Game House window or out back lying back on a lounge chair under the sun? They would kill to be a Playboy Centerfold.

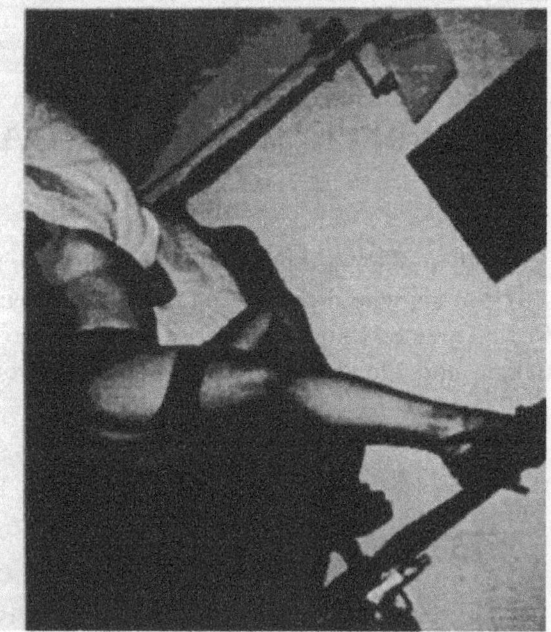

Courtesy John Dante, private collection

4: JOHN DANTE'S LAST ORGASM

"I started smoking a joint and did a little coke then the girls came out. They, of course, would concentrate on Hef. Their main interest was to get Hef off. Three or four would work on him. Barry would have a girl he'd be fucking and Quint would have his and I would have mine."—John Dante

They were in the Game House.

"It was a night when we were playing backgammon, and Hef said, 'We're having a thing tonight.' "

"Who else is involved?" he had the presence of mind to ask.

The Mansion orgy, according to John Dante, unlike a baseball team, did not have a regular lineup. Personnel of a particular orgy at a particular time depended on which corps of favorite women of fantastic beauty and generosity happened to be populating their lives at the time.

Hef answered, "Well, Barry [porn star] is going to be there, and Quint…"

"Aw, hell," he muttered to himself. "I didn't like to be in a scene with Quint. He was like a goat in heat. He was a pounder. There was nothing delicate about him, and he was a turn-off. So I almost declined, almost said, 'I think I'll pass,' but I didn't."

Except for his mother and perhaps Shel Silverstein, there hadn't been anyone in his life as steadfast as Hef. He filled out the roster of John Dante's Last Orgy, which included six women and a former high school friend of one of the women.

He said to himself: "Somebody new. It might be interesting." Then to Hef he said, "OK," and the orgy was on.

It was to be the kind of orgy that Shel had in mind John should write about, the kind of orgy that Playboy enthusiasts imagine: healthy, happy, rollicking, generous, gorgeous, free beautiful women with great bodies—all making love. The quintessential mansion orgy, like those he and Hef had shared throughout the 40 years of their friendship, in like spirit, taking their time, loving their women, their women loving them. An orgy consisting of more women than men, sustained pairing off not occurring until the orgy's twilight. Maybe that's the reason John listed this orgy late on the Sunday of his one weekend—he could lose himself in the reverie of drugs and sex and loving two, three, four, an infinite number of women, all at the same time, and know, just know that Hef was there, too. Six girls and four guys, enough to go around, enough to revel in, to leave life in.

courtesy John Dante, private collection

"Vrrooomm!" the Playboy jet's rear-fuselage, mounted jet engines rev up. Moving, he had to keep moving. When the fallen angels carrying bows and arrows herd you to be judged before the bearded demon Minos of the wraparound tail, you are naked and you are ashamed of your nudity so you cower and attempt to hide your shame by covering your fig, like Venus covering hers with her snaking, flaming hair. That's why he opted for cremation—his private as well as public parts would be reduced to ash. The second lesson he remembered from the Benedictine monks was that, once you are dumped and land with a thud in your appropriate Circle and Bolge, you cannot move, you cannot get out, again like the Gluttons which are unable to move away from the thundering din and pelting hailstones and fast-moving rain. Picking up speed on the runway and then the black DC-9 lifts off and slices up through the clouds.

To Africa, Ginger Miles in his arms with the black night sky fixed with stars and the moon outside their window, aboard with Hef and film director Roman Polanski, whose beloved wife and precious eight-month-old son were murdered in their home on Cielo Drive in Benedict Canyon, Los Angeles. Their killers up to the hairline in Hell's River of Blood. He stands with Hef and Polanski on the expansive savannah, in bush khakis and helmets, Polanski holding a camera, framing a shot. His wife was interred with their son in her arms. To Venice—someone in the prow of their gondola captured Hef at a moment when he was happy, arm around his special lady, pipe in mouth, wearing the same chiaroscuro striped shirt as the gondolier, who rows and guides with his long oar along a residential lagoon leading into the St. Mark basin. All smiling broadly—what was just ahead that captured their attention so raptly? Carnival, masked revelers approaching? At that one costume party dressed as a sailor, Hef beside him looking like a crusading knight, both unmasked, in costume yet recognized as so much the couple. They visited his hometown of Fossacesia, where the language came back to him and his pride in being Italian in America was awakened, and he and Hef probably strolled by his first small house in which his mother nurtured and protected him and then took him to America when he was two, to join her husband with the heart of a poet.

The backgammon game ended at the approach of deep night. An exciting, expectant silence pervaded the Mansion. The women were upstairs, preparing.

"They prepared themselves like there was going to be a shoot: make-up, perfume, garter belts. In short, dress up."

One of the women prepared Hef's bedroom.

"She lined up the music—" he was reading a new biography of Cole Forster one of the last times we spoke—"and lit the incense and took out the toys, dildos and vibrators and dope (coke and grass). Hef went upstairs and took Barry and Quint with him, and I went to my room. Barry and Quint didn't live in the Mansion so they just went upstairs and took off their clothes and put on robes. I took a shower and put on a little cologne and my robe."

A Stroke of Good Luck

John Dante may have been one of the few who witnessed Hugh Hefner scream, fly into a jealous rage, lower his head in despair and cry. In their privacy, the great friends must have grieved and consoled one another on the passing of loved ones, family, friends, the departure of a cherished lover. John Dante knew the Hugh Hefner other than the one who, for the most part, appears in a three-piece, vested suit or a pair of silk pajamas, pipe in hand, free arm around a young, voracious, beautiful lady. But then, in the mid-1980s, slowly, unseen, and unfelt until the blossoming of symptoms, a number of Hef's brain cells began to die.

Around the time John returned from Taos and Hef not only forgave him but wanted him to stay at home more than before, John hired a manager for the Touch club.

"It wasn't the same," says Noel Cunningham. "It missed John's touch."

But John stayed at home because Hef wanted him to, and he went through the motions of playing cards and watching movies and, on

Thursday nights, transformed half-heartedly into a pig. In time, Touch's manager did not work out, and John returned to the helm.

"I couldn't just walk away, because if I wasn't there, there was nobody there. Hef didn't give a shit whether the place ran down the toilet. He was more interested that I wasn't going to be in the house."

Apparently, Hef did not feel that Touch was the way to his, and Playboy's, future, unless his love for John and need to have him at home superseded any role Touch could play.

There could be slow, long, dreamy days filled with sunshine, love and lust, and there could be times when momentous events coalesced into a single moment. The latter was now such a time.

In 1984, the esteemed film director Peter Bogdonovitch published *The Killing of the Unicorn,* a book which documents the author's love and longing for the tragic victim, Dorothy Stratten. Bogdonovitch loved and was in love with Ms. Stratten at the time of her murder, and she him. Perhaps, assigning blame, however tangential and inferior to that love, seemed like a just thing to do on behalf of the victim and may also have assuaged temporarily the aggrieved lover's sense of heart-breaking loss. Fault floats and slivers in thin air, impossible to harness. The lover can blame the power broker. The *Village Voice* Pulitzer-Prize winning writer can blame the both of them. Soft Ice Cream could not have been totally at fault. He was such a minor character and player, a hustler and a pimp, that, set against Ms. Stratten's extraordinary beauty, intelligence and talent, he was not worthy of blame. Before blowing his own head away, the killer left a note, blaming neither Bogdonovitch nor Hefner nor himself, but rather two of his friends "for not keeping a closer eye on me."

In 1985, Hef suffered a "mild" stroke. Did John notice Hef beginning to have trouble walking or speaking, or hear him complain of headaches? Did he console and care for him? Maybe Shel Silverstein had in mind that John's personal relationship with Hef was as worthy of literature, of writing about, as his experience and knowledge of Playboy's inner workings and its women. As a mark of the great friendship between John and Hef, John's impulse was to respond with venom like a lioness over her threatened cubs to any finger pointing to Hef that he had anything to do with Dorothy Stratten's tragic death. The way he told Hef straight up, John was out to tell posterity straight up in his notes from Hell, which were already a kind of book whose audience were Hell's shades, as well as the stultifying air of his ramshackle bungalow and the frisky poodles and the mountain of snuffed-out cigarettes in his ashtray that sat on his sticky Formica dinette table.

"In my opinion, Dorothy Stratten was murdered by her jealous husband because of the affair she was having. A few years later, a book came out that insinuated blame for her death on Hef. The book was probably the main cause of the stroke that Hef suffered."

The medical profession aptly describes stroke symptoms and how they occur, but only John Dante knew the exact etiology of Hef's mild stroke. Not the book or its author but the very shadow of insinuation—he had witnessed Hef's anguish over Miss Stratten's brutal murder. The gruesome, transformative images after her murder that assaulted Hef set beside images of one of the most beautiful, popular, and nicest Playmate in the history of Playboy—according to John Dante, all of this acted as weight on Hef's blood vessels, constricting them, with consequent reduction of oxygen flow to his brain.

Hef may have termed his minor stroke without ostensible deficits a "stroke of good luck" because it caused him to reset his priorities in life, which, in turn, could very well stave off a second stroke, a major one, and it gave him another chance to love and be loved. Hold back the pressure in his heart and in his arteries and veins by cutting back, say, on all-night pool parties and orgies. Plain and simple—he was about to turn 60 years of age, maybe it was time to settle down. Hef arrived at a juncture that John had reached a decade before and rejected, or, it had rejected him: take a wife and, if she wished, have children. He would preserve his remaining heartbeats. It was also about time he cleaned house.

"After four-and-a-half years in operation, just when Touch was becoming extremely popular, Hef and I had a few spats about personal matters and he ordered Touch sold."

Spats over personal matters: opting to take his father to Taos instead of staying at home? Going back to work at Touch? Having first-time prostitutes over when there were so many beautiful women in the house already? No-Bullshit John confronting Hef—not necessarily about himself, that they could have slowed down and grown old together but about his up-coming marriage? Marriage was so much out of character. Hadn't they both rejected the bourgeois institution, about which his great forefather Casanova had said: "Marriage is the tomb of love."

About the closing of the Touch club, Noel Cunningham says:

"All John wanted was the plaque on the door of a man and a woman dancing, touching, and he gave it to me. I'm a better man and a better chef for knowing John. I thought I'd had good training, but John fine-tuned it. My restaurants are successful because of the details he taught me. I missed Touch for five years after it closed. I'd give up my restaurants in a heartbeat for that place to continue on."

The Memoirs of Casanova, illustrated by M. Blaine

The handsome castrato Bellino upon whom Casanova staked his reputation that (s)he was really a woman agreed to travel with him as far as Senegalia. It was deep in the night so they dismounted at the post-house inn and unloaded their trunks, then Casanova secured a decent room and ordered dinner. To Casanova's discerning eye, in the manner of Bellino's speech, the expression in his eyes, and his smiles, he seemed like a different person. Guessing that they were at the denouement of their romance, Casanova terminated dinner early, and they went to their room. There was one bed.

"Would you like me to light a fire in another room?" Casanova asked Bellino with deference.

To which Bellino replied gently, "I do not mind sleeping in your bed."

Casanova writes: "If I found myself in the right that Bellino was a woman, I could expect the most precious favors."

Bellino called for a night lamp, undressed and got into bed. Casanova, naked as a babe, followed. Nothing suffices better than the authentic voices of men of such august stature as the great lovers John Dante and Casanova de Seingalt.

"She came close to me the moment I was in bed. Without uttering a word, our lips met, and I found myself in ecstasy. I could not take my eyes off that beautiful face, which was aflame with the ardor of love. Bellino was out to make me forget my sufferings and to reward me with an ardor equal to the fire kindled by her charms. The happiness that I gave to her increased mine two-fold, for it has always been my weakness to compose the four-fifths of my enjoyment from the sum total of the happiness which I give to the charming being from whom I derived it."

Her name was Teresa and, during a repose, she got out of bed, poured a little water in a cup, opened her trunk, and took out her "device" and its glue that she used to deceive the inspecting priests who looked from the door or front of the foot of the bed as to her sex. The device was, Casanova describes—"…a sort of flabby, long tube about as thick as a human thumb with very soft, white skin. The tube is attached to a thin, transparent oval of skin 5 or 6 inches long and about 2 inches wide. This skin is then applied with gum dragon to the area of the female sex organ. Now Teresa melted the glue and applied the camouflage. I saw then a girl whose charm was visible in all her person, but who, with that white appendage, looked even more appealing to me, for it posed no obstacle to the reservoir of her sex.

" 'You were right,' I told her, 'not to let me touch it, for it would have plunged me into a drunken state…' " The give and take became comical. "Playing, making torrid love with the device still attached."

…Wearing his own in-house, lush, white Orgy robe, and with his Cologne wafting into the Mansion air, he went up to Hef's bedroom for the last time.

"Hef, Quint, and Barry were sitting on the bed, smoking a joint…" The opulent orgy surface of Hef's bed which he had lain on for 26 years—TV cameras, headboard controls for the music and vibrators, carved wood, statues of women all around, awaiting their counterparts in the human flesh—was still so familiar. "They were waiting for me." The men waited for the girls to come out, and they also waited for John to come up. Hef, Quint, and countless other good men down through the years could not imagine a Mansion orgy without John and the beautiful women he brought to it when he was at home.

"I started smoking a joint and did a little coke, then the girls came out. They, of course, would concentrate on Hef. Their main interest was to get Hef off. Barry would have a girl he'd be fucking, Quint would have his, and I would have mine. Three or four would work on Hef."

A BOOK

John Dante divined correctly that, at the end of his life in Playboy, old and withered, whether he was still living with Hef in the Mansion or in a villa in Florence or alone with the poodles, only his memories would be left to him and he would capitalize on these memories by writing a book. He came up with a working title, *Guest at the Party*. Despite working with Hef and cohabitating with him—breathing the same air, sleeping and loving often the same women under the same roof for 25 odd years—still, he felt like a guest, no different than a Playboy Bunny who returned to the Mansion after her tour and then left, or a Playmate who was assigned a room for a few weeks during her tests and shoots and then, one day, left. And he knew what he would do with his book's advance and royalties:

"I want to live out my life in a dignified way in Italy, land of my birth, specifically in Florence, birthplace of my great forefather, Dante Alighieri."

But he felt that he needed help with the writing because the emotions that these memories invoked were powerful and swirling, like the gale winds that toss the Lustful hither and yon. The images terrible and delectable arising from these memories, combined with the complex, nuanced characters and reigning in and organizing the long haul of time—all overwhelmed him. Also, his book should be written in English, for Playboy was an American phenomenon, but English was his second language. From the age of two to the age of eight, he got by in Chicago by "mimicking. If I saw that the speaker was laughing, I'd laugh. If I noticed a pair of lips curled in anger, I grew angry."

He was like a ventriloquist's dummy, and the Americans around him whose faces and lips he was attempting to read were the ventriloquists. In time, his English was devoid of accent, and he became well-spoken, reflecting the style of his fiber, and his voice grew stentorian and his words rang peremptorily, like the monsignor's of his parish—John Dante, Monsignor of Sex! But his vocabulary lacked the scope for a book that should reflect his vast, rich experience. He began taking notes in his room in the Mansion, handwritten on yellow legal pads with a black marker, using em dashes for punctuation, just the way Silverstein wrote. Shel was always writing and sketching any place where he could find a sugar bowl. John's handwriting of clear, perfectly formed scripted letters practiced over and over stemmed from his Catholic grammar and high school education during the 1940s and '50s, which relied on rote memory to learn. But there was nothing rote or wooden or mannequin-like about Susan Einway or Katherine Forster or Linda Lovelace or the thousands of women in his private scenes and in the orgies. Rote it was not to see, to smell, to touch each and every "10" of the approximately 16,000 "10s". Each could have effused Je Reviens and worn seamed stockings and high heels—and still would have been different. He needed a literary arsenal to move among these differences. There was something else—the Polaroids. Over the years, he snapped about 20 thousand, each one-time snapshot capturing a lover in seamed stockings and high heels, and he had carried his Polaroids in transfer cases from Chicago to Los Angeles, and kept adding to them. Even if nothing ever changed, Hef and him sitting before a warm, consoling fire, they would flip through the Polaroids and he would recall a particular night with a particular lover. But then, one of Hef's former lovers asked him to destroy the videos of their sex together, and he complied. John Dante could be provocative. The every-day, business-as-usual, sex-in-the-Mansion for him could be extraordinary to the layman—exactly what Shel Silverstein well understood and urged John to exploit—so when he told me about this prominent personality's request and Hef's granting of it, I asked John, assuming correctly that he had viewed the torrid videos:

"How was the sex between them?"

He looked away, in his memory rewound those videos, and, viewing them, began shaking his head, slowly. He turned back and said nothing.

At the same time, a former lover of his asked him to destroy the Polaroids, and he complied.

"When I told Shel I had deep-sixed the Polaroids, he said, 'Why?' "

Some thousands of photographs of John Dante's lovers sleep with the fishes. Now he had to find the language of associating the curvature of a calf or cuneiform bone prominence or shape of an inner thigh or the style and color of a pair of high heel shoes, with a particular night and a particular lover.

"Did you destroy all of the Polaroids?" I asked him.

"No. But this time I told them to cover their faces."

He termed taking Polaroid snapshots of his lovers a "nefarious hobby." He wrote in his last letter to me:

"I know that it must seem perverse (and I hope Victoria [my special lady] doesn't think me a 'pig' before meeting me) but—no harm was ever done—it was very erotic and stimulating fore-play–and the ladies actually enjoyed doing it—because it aroused me so much—and I was able to preserve these 'fantasy nights'. With the pictures I was able to re-call a particular night with a particular person."

He decided to write his book himself, with help.

"I enrolled in a writing course at U.C.L.A."

Gustav Doré's THE DESCENT OF THE MONSTER GERYON
"Slowly, slowly, swimming, he moves on;
he wheels and he descends, but I feel only the wind upon my face and the wind rising." (Inf. XVII, 115, 116, 117)

…" 'Aaahhhh…' Hef starts coming. I'm on top of Nancy fucking her and Barry and Quint are doing their thing, and I remember Annie and Dolores and the new girl Alice were working on Hef. All of a sudden, he starts coming, "Aaaaahhhhh…' I hadn't come yet, Quint must have come three or four times already and, as Hef was coming, the girls start saying: 'C'mon, baby. C'mon, Hef…' "

He began attending his writing classes at U.C.L.A. and doing his homework of exercises and writing on his yellow legal pads a list of the highlights of his life in Playboy, including the scene between Linda Lovelace and Rufus in the Bath House, The Murder of Dorothy Stratten and its effects on Hef, the story of the rise and fall of the Touch Club, and his affair with his grammar school teacher. Thus, he began preliminary work on his book while living in Los Angeles in his home, the Playboy Mansion, the way his great forefather Dante began writing *The Divine Comedy* while living in Florence in his home with his wife and children, sketching 7 of the 34 cantos before his exile for the crime of Barratry, acts of fraud against the public trust. So deep and dark in Hell does Dante place the Barrators, Circle 8 Bolge 5, that he and his guide Virgil cannot get down there themselves, the way from the Sodomites to the Barrators treacherous going, what with a series of vast, steep cliffs and a pitch black pit below. What is needed is transportation in the form of a winged beast—here comes Geryon, Monster of Fraud, crawling out of the sea with its three heads and three conjoined bodies with wings and the face of an honest man but the body of a wyvern with its hairy paws, reptilian hide, and poisonous scorpion's tail. Dante and Virgil climb onto Geryon's back and, terrified, spin down and around into strong headwinds, to the black depths of the Barrators. Perhaps this is his forebear's great final act—placing himself in a Hell of his own creation before he arrived there, in the deepest, blackest pit. The two Dantes would share the hell of Hell, each in their respective circle and pit. Elder Dante had to write his book before he could place himself in Hell. Yes, before his sinful soul could be saved, he had to write a book in which he travels through Hell, up through Purgatory, then up to Paradise, at the same time leaving behind his place in Circle 8 Bolge 5 in the lake of boiling pitch. Before modern Dante could live out his days in Florence, then, most likely, suffer forever in Circle 2 of the Lustful, lashed and blown topsy-turvy through the black air, crying out, along with other fallen great lovers, such as Francesca and Paolo, Cleopatra, Helen of Troy, and Tristan—first he had to write his book.

But then Geryon's poisonous tail snapped and struck—his creative writing course conflicted with the Wednesday night UNO card game which began promptly at eight p.m., and he was expected to play. Mansion ritual had its innate strictures, the way games of chance have their immutable rules. Lovers come and go, but the card game endures. If a regular UNO player was missing (*uno* is the Italian word for "one") but still alive, the game was simply not the same. *Uno* loses *uno's* spot in the card group upon dying.

The card game UNO was invented in 1971 by a Hungarian barber, Merle Robbins, who went on to make a fortune, collecting ten cents for each of the millions of UNO decks manufactured. If he, author John Dante, could collect $.10 royalty on each copy of *Guest at the Party* sold worldwide, he could support himself and Hef in Florence, in a cozy villetta at the base of the Senese Clavey Hills, near the Boboli Gardens. In UNO, the player who has discarded all of his or her cards is declared the victor. A player with nothing wins—rare in the Playboy or any other type of world—but the player holding a penultimate card must be vigilante of his own possessions and announce, "Uno!" to alert the other players that a sole card remains. If such a player does not declare "Uno!" and another player notices, the player with lapsed memory forfeits.

That's another reason why he needed help with his book—in the event of lapses in his memory, since he lived his life as though he was not going to write about it.

Instead of the Hungarian word for one, "Egy!" Merle Robbins may have named his card game after the Italian because he well understood how Italian card games like scopa and briscola, in cultivating the arts of concealment and entrapment, are passed down through the generations. Hef probably knew that the game rang of the Italian and that his best friend was born Giovanni Aimola and that the elders on Chicago's west side taught Italian card games to the boys. In short, John Dante was the House Italian. John Dante was Hef's Italian uncircumcised self. John Dante was the Italian closest to Hef over the course of his entire lifetime, and only John's familiar, articulate, baritone voice could utter the word "Uno" correctly. "U-u-u-u..." pressing and extending the first vowel sound, in the manner of an owl or as an exclamation of surprise or effusion of ecstasy or reaction to sudden pain. And then, lingering on the "n" as if it echoed—"n-n-n"—culminating with an abrupt "o", like a last hiccup.

"U-u-u-u-n-n-n-o!" only John could announce correctly, holding his penultimate card.

Such is their insistence on lust instead of love that the Lustful of Circle 2, frozen in their raging desire, cannot move, so Hef must be on the move, the *padrone* descending the same stairwell as had the glowing Haley four or five times, she in pink peignoir, seamed stockings, and high heels, now Hef in black silk pajamas, holding a vintage pipe between his lips, and he alights gingerly outside of John's room. Then he goes in and mentions the upcoming UNO game on Wednesday night. John tells him:

"I can't play UNO on Wednesday, because I have to do my homework."

Hef "looked downtrodden and he got pissed off because my schooling took away from my time with him."

Were not the passing years strung with beautiful women and the faces of mutual friends and Aces and Queens and crinkling cash bills and clanking backgammon cubes and pinballs and heavy breaths and hoof beats of thoroughbred horses—all swirling tumbling tinkling careening topsy-turvy up to the present? Why, Don Adams has been coming to the Mansion to play gin rummy for 20 years. After he dropped off copies of *Playboy* in the clubs along Rush Street, and after Dante's Inferno with a two o-clock license closed, hadn't they all gone over to Milano's for breakfast and played Liar's Poker, using the serial numbers on dollar bills, while the gangsters, sitting against the wall, waved and greeted them?

Hef may not have been receptive to downers, still, he repeated:

"Sorry, but I have to do my exercises."

Hef left, closing the door behind him.

"A few days later, he told me that, when he left my room, he cried."

He could not bear the thought of his best friend crying. He could not withstand the guilt that he was the one who caused his friend to shed tears. The way Beatrice in Paradise heard the anguish of Dante's cry from Hell, he heard the anguish of Hef's tears shed over him outside his room. He gave up his writing course at U.C.L.A.

"I was one of his prize possessions."

This was the third event that made him feel like a possession of Hef's. First, taking his father out of the nursing home to a home in Taos as a way of alleviating his guilt. Second, the Touch club, Hef wanting him to stay at home regardless of the stakes. Now his writing course at

U.C.L.A. Acceding to Hef's desire to stay at home under the rubric of gambling reduced him to chattel, to some owned mindless thing, the way in Chicago they had considered songstress Billie Nelson a piece of common chattel they could all boff. He was no more human than a pair of rare Madeira silk pajamas, sucked and puffed like a FreeHand pipe. Prize chattel in the vein of the great Venetian painter Titian's triptych of Saint Sebastian, the patron saint of fags. In the vein of the wooden shoe with shiny brass buckle worn by Captain Bradford, Hef's original American ancestor. An artichoke just like his homeland of Italy, plucked leaf by leaf by invading foreign powers.

Time passed with him believing that he was not up to the literary task of writing his own book. The Mansion mates Hef, Shel, and John grew older, while a fresh supply of Bunnies and Playmates and models and actresses and women who were merely 7s and 8s kept coming, forever youthful and beautiful, skin smooth and taut. There was no room in Playboy for an aged Playmate or Playboy. Bunnies and Playmates and playboys grow old, each in their own way, in some other place. A stroke of Hugh Hefner's genius was to create a world of perennially youthful beauty. A cruel Dorian Gray twist of fate for John Dante in that the picture's artist, Hugh Hefner, remains unafflicted, while his man of parts for decades, 40 years to be precise, 26 of those years living together in the Mansion, the man who helped build the Playboy empire, is powerless, filled with doubt, and declines irreparably.

"…And Hef's going, 'Aaaaahhhhh…' Even Nancy who I was fucking is saying, 'C'mon, Hef. C'mon…' I'm fucking her and she's ignoring me. I'm fucking her and she's going, 'C'mon, Hef…' "

Dante's She-Wolf who guards the way to the foot of the mountain that leads to Paradise and Beatrice does not have to tell the poet of her terrible internal and external power. Hef did not have to tell him to leave in so many words for him to know. Hef got married, and the Mansion was the newlyweds' home.

Hef's marriage baffled John to the end of his days. It was as if Hef got married again and again every time he thought back to it, as if Hef was telling him time and again that he was taking another, a woman, in matrimony.

"I just don't understand it. Here's a man who's been to the mountaintop and he gets married," John told me down in Florida when I asked him why he left the Mansion. At first, he and the bride did not get along, John continued, but then they became friends, and she was kind to him. As long as a Mrs. Hefner was living in the Mansion, he may have felt uncomfortable having hookers come to the front gate, and he had squandered the money and property his mother had bequeathed to him, also the house in Taos. The reason for leaving could simply have been, as Noel Cunningham puts it—

"When there are three in a relationship, one has to go."

The groom carries his bride over the threshold, and another man is living in the house.

He heard about a bungalow down in Fort Lauderdale that he could use. The silver Isuzu could make it, and he would go with the poodles, for only his love for them and their love for him remained steadfast.

Last moments of John Dante's One Weekend of Ecstasy:

"…all of a sudden—'Yeeeaaaahhh!' Hef comes. I keep fucking Nancy because I want to get off, too. But she sidles out of me and looks at me, as if to say: 'Hey, man, you know the rules—when Hef comes, it's over.' The procedure was that, after Hef came, he ordered food from downstairs: burgers, hot dogs, whatever anybody wanted, including champagne. I'm left with a hard-on, and Hef is on the phone ordering himself a grilled cheese sandwich and malted milk. He asks everybody, 'OK, what do you want?' Nancy calls out, 'I'll have a cheeseburger and a coke!' "

Los Angeles, 1993

It was early morning, about the time an orgy ended, the birds in the aviary heralding a new day and the yellow sun peeking onto Los Angeles, and John Dante tiptoes over the driveway cobbles. God forbid Hef is watching from a top-floor window, lace curtain drawn aside.

"Sh-h-h, Looie, Pepper…"

The poodles yap, tails wagging, ears pricked, and jump through the silver Isuzu's passenger side window and position themselves side by side, paws up, tongues out, heads thrust out. He loads little more than the one battered suitcase his mother had carried from their homeland of Italy. Steerage in, steerage out. Only the day before, he'd had a couple-of-hundred-dollar stake.

"How the fuck are you going to exist on this?" he said to himself in perfect English. That's hardly enough for dog food and gas to Texas, let alone Fort Lauderdale. So, as always, he gambled. He went with Don Adams to Hollywood Park and won $25,000.

"Don drove. When we got back to the Mansion—it was a Tuesday, because on Wednesday we had our card game which Don was part of—I said, 'I'm going to say goodbye to you now.'

"Don said, 'What do you mean goodbye? Where the fuck are you going?'

" 'I'm leaving the Mansion.' "

Into the driver's seat, buckle up. Los Angeles down through San Diego, San Antonio, Houston, Tampa—it was all the same to the poodles. Three thousand miles of cool, rustling breeze.

Before he left the Mansion, he wrote a letter to Shel Silverstein. They had been friends for 40 years, since the time of Dante's Inferno and, especially, of his Bunny Hunts, when he had brought some of the women back home, two on each arm, smiling, whistling an Italian tune.

"Ladies, say hello to Hef. Oh, and this is Shel Silverstein."

This is the precise time when he and Shel became friends.

"I brought back some great-looking chics that Shel was privy to, that he got to. Then we became friends."

It was not only that for the first time in his life Shel had access to several beautiful women at one and the same time, or that he became the lover of one or a few. When he was around 13, 14 years of age, he tried hard to excel at baseball, but he wasn't a good player. To be around the game, he got a job selling hot dogs in Comiskey Park, where he may have handed a frankfurter or two to John Dante's old nemesis, Hot Dog Lasciandrello, and may have gotten the idea for *Three Eyes*, the baffled man with a third eye in the center of his forehead. Nor was teenage Shelly a hit with the girls, he couldn't dance, but he accepted who he was, a non-athletic boy whom the girls didn't shine to. With the benefit of hindsight, he considered himself fortunate because he could throw himself into his drawing and his writing. Maybe girls would come later on, and later on, too, maybe he could get a box seat at Comiskey Park. Beautiful women came to the house on the arms of John Dante, giving him a chance, some time with an attractive woman so that his charm and his wit and his humor and his generosity and his capacity to love could shine through. Perhaps this is what Shel was eternally grateful to John Dante for, the prime reason he sought to help him, including with his book, more so than paltry ecstatic moments of his one weekend of bliss—John gave him the opportunity and the time for a woman to like, even love, him.

John did not say whether he left the letter for Shel in the Mansion or mailed it, if at all, to one of Shel's myriad addresses, for he gave me the original. The Key West season began in October, maybe Shel was in his house on Jane Street, sitting on his porch, barefoot, guitar in hand, humming a tune. Or maybe he was still in his apartment in Greenwich Village, smoking a cigar at his desk, then working at an Italian Café, under a Cinzano umbrella. Here is John's letter, dated October 18, 1991:

Hey Shel—

Well—I'm finally leaving—maybe not quite the way I wanted to—but I don't think it could have happened any other way. I got too hooked on the "Life"—totally drugged out on Lotus Blossoms.

It's funny—when a woman decides to turn "pro" it's referred to as going into "The Life." Interesting correlation.

I tried to think of ways to break away and become self-reliant again—but I guess I've just become too weak to do it. What's it called? Losing your "Chops"?

Anyway, I've finally come to the end of my time and finances and now I have got to preserve what little dignity I may have left. Italians have this thing about dignity.

However—I want you to know a few of my thoughts and feelings before leaving because I'll probably not get the chance to talk to you again.

I think of it this way: I've gambled all my life and I've never quit while I was ahead—I'm going to do that now—that is—quit while I'm ahead in the game of life. I don't see the coming years as being all that great whereas the years I've had have been pretty wonderful. Matter of fact I'm kind of anxious and curious to go into the "whatever"—kind of like a lost adventure.

There are a few people I'm going to miss—and one of them, of course, is you. Maybe you most of all.

Dante Alighieri (1265-1321) died in exile in Ravenna of malaria, asweat, with insatiable thirst, after completing the last part, "Paradiso," of his great epic poem, *The Divine Comedy.* Though hundreds of miles from his hometown of Florence and his wife and children, at least in his work he attained Paradise and his Beatrice and saw the face of God. Dante was buried in Ravenna's Church of San Pietro Maggiore. His friend Bernardo Canaccio wrote a verse on the grave dedicated not to the Supreme Poet himself but to his beloved homeland of Florence:

Parvi Florentia mater amoris.
Florence, mother of little love.

Five hundred years later, the city of Florence built a cenotaph in Dante's honor in the basilica of Santa Croce with the inscription:

Onorate l'ultissimmo poeta
Honor the most exalted poet.

Giacomo Casanova

Casanova de Seingalt (1725-1798) died in exile in Bohemia (Czech Republic) while serving as librarian to Count Joseph Karl von Waldstein, chamberlain of the emperor. At his death, Casanova was still at work on his multi-volume memoir written in his second language of French, entitled *Histoire de ma vie.* The great philosopher, lover, and predecessor to Rodolpho Valentino and John Dante wrote not to better his situation, rather, as "the sole remedy to keep from going mad or dying of grief." Casanova was buried in a small cemetery behind his last refuge, Duchov Castle. Years later, a park was constructed out of the cemetery so that, above Casanova's remains, for centuries now, children have run and played.

Rodolfo Valentino (1895-1926) died of acute peritonitis in Polyclinic Hospital, New York City. A thousand women waited in the rain under a sea of black umbrellas to view Valentino's body in the bronze catafalque in Frank E. Campbell Funeral Chapel. Mounted police in wet leather jackets and caps tried to rein in the crowd maddened with grief. Women feinted. Some committed suicide. Others broke through the chapel's glass window to get a glimpse of the Great Lover, a man they had not touched or heard or even seen in the flesh. Valentino's body was taken by train across the United States and buried in Hollywood Forever Cemetery.

Shel Silverstein (1930-1999). On the spring day of his death, May 9th, in his home in Key West, Florida, his good friend of 40 years John Dante was on his way to see him. That morning I spoke to John:

"He got up and it hit him. Heart attack."

Often from across the street of his house on Hudson Street, New York City, I look across and up at his second-storey windows and whisper, "Shel…" That mild spring night, I laid a bouquet in the corner of his front doorstep, in behalf of myself and Dusty LaBelle.

Sheldon Allan Silverstein was buried in Westlawn Cemetery, Cook County, Illinois. His inscription reads:

"Beloved Father, Brother, Uncle and Friend."

Florence. Photo by Anthony Valerio

John Dante (1928-2003) died in the Florida Keys. Shel, myself, Frank D'Rone, Noel Cunningham, and unknown others kept in touch with John after he left the Mansion. Musician and singer extraordinaire Frank D'Rone says that, one day after John died, a woman called him but would not give her name. She could have been a woman John had met in Florida or any one of the thousands of women he had loved who continued to love him pursuant to his life in Playboy. Frank relays what this mystery woman told him, leaving a few details to the imagination.

A singular woman who has retained her great style and beauty passes her shoulder bag through airport security on the American side. She does not want to be questioned about the urn, secure and warm in a cache of soft clothing. She does not want to exhibit her lingerie, her seamed stockings. She does not want to lie that the urn is filled with homegrown oregano. Her bag passes through without attention, and she boards and sits and buckles up, clutching her carry-on. Her warm hands enfold it 30,000 feet over the Atlantic, then through the change in time zone, six hours ahead in Italy. The descent is long and slow. The snaking Arno River comes into view, and then the sandstone of the Duomo Cathedral's dome beams the golden color of the midday sun reflected in the air and the soil. The low, undulating Senese Clavey hills seem to caress the great Renaissance City. Tears well up as she checks in, showers and dresses up in a white corset dress, seamed stockings, high heels, and a black bonnet. Cradling the urn, she walks to the Duomo and spreads some ashes in the piazza, thronged with tourists from around the world. She walks with her head high and a sure step, her tears making a chiaroscuro of smeared black mascara on fair skin, to the Piazza della Signoria, spreading more ashes as she goes. Michelangelo's David is a replica here so she goes over to view the original, housed in the Galleria del'Accademia, ashes spilling though her elegant fingers onto the corridor floor of the master sculptor's unfinished Bound Slaves, and then more ashes spill while she stands in awe and sadness behind the glass of the original, mighty David. Over to the bustling Ponte Vecchio lined with artisans' shops, where she presses against the stone barrier, and ashes dandle onto the surface of the Arno, like virgin snowflakes the size of quarters. She watches until his ashes become one with Italian water. Then to the end of this bridge, where young Dante waited for Beatrice to pass on the evening stroll just to have a look at her. Their small chapel is small, intimate, and silent, yet you could hear the thunderclaps of their grand, eternal, unrequited love, Dante able to glimpse her only from the last row through a maze of parishioners' heads, Beatrice feeling his heart on the nape of her neck. Ashes drop onto the kneeler and marble floor below. The sun is setting, and the climb up the hill is gradual and arduous. At the summit, she looks out and, through the jutting trees, at the magnificent city, home to Dante, Michelangelo, Leonardo da Vinci, and now, John Dante. She has never before seen the quality of this light. A soft, roseate light that seems to kiss and fuse with the red terracotta roof tiles and the very air. Caste by the setting sun, yet the light seems to emanate from all that is material in the great city. A warm, touching glow, as from an embrace. With a flourish, her entire body animating, the Last Woman Who Loved John Dante raises her arm–and tosses all that remains of him out and up into the beautiful, oncoming Florentine night.

John Dante, private collection

Easter Sunday, 2012. AV

Anthony Valerio is the author of ten books of fiction and nonfiction. His short stories have appeared in the Paris Review and in readers and anthologies published by Random House, William Morrow and the Viking Press. He was a book editor in major publishing houses, including McGraw-Hill. Mr. Valerio has taught writing at NYU, CUNY and Wesleyan University. He was a fiction judge on PEN's Prison Writing Committee and is a member of the Author's Guild.

Anthony Valerio 20/20

Anthony Valerio is the author of ten books of fiction and nonfiction. His short stories have appeared in the Paris Review and in reviews and anthologies published by Random House, William Morrow and the Viking Press. He was a book editor in major publishing houses, including McGraw-Hill. Mr. Valerio has taught writing at NYU, CUNY and Wesleyan University. He was a fiction judge on PEN's Prison Writing Committee and is a member of the Authors Guild.

CPSIA information can be obtained
at www.ICGtesting.com
Printed in the USA
LVHW101039180322
713776LV00003B/141

9 780990 467526